Jesus' People

Jesus' People

What the Church should do next

S<small>TEVEN</small> C<small>ROFT</small>

CHURCH HOUSE
PUBLISHING

Church House Publishing
Church House
Great Smith Street
London SW1P 3AZ

ISBN 978 0 7151 4300 1

Published 2009 by Church House Publishing
Copyright © Steven Croft 2009
Second impression 2012

Printed in England by CPI Group (UK) Ltd., Croydon, CR0 4YY

Contents

Convictions

Over the last five years I have been on a journey, exploring what it means to be church in the twenty-first century. This short book contains my conclusions. We are living in a time of immense change. As a Church we need to become more like Jesus. We need to live by the priorities of Jesus. We will only find the strength to change if we are deeply rooted in the life of Jesus. We are called to be Jesus' people.

In one sense I have been on a journey for the whole of my life exploring what it means to be church. But this part of the journey began in 2004 when I was invited to set up and lead a new initiative called Fresh Expressions on behalf of the Archbishops and the Methodist Council. The role of Fresh Expressions is to encourage mission through new forms of church for our changing culture.

Almost immediately I began travelling across the country, listening to what is happening to the Church across Great Britain and beyond. I have covered tens of thousands of miles by rail and road and occasionally by air. I've listened to pioneers in Exeter and archdeacons in Newcastle. I've spoken with lay people in Carlisle and clergy in Canterbury and everything in between. I've spent time with high church folk and with low church, with Roman Catholics and Salvationists, with those who think we should abandon the idea of church altogether and with those who think we should go back to the way things were.

At the end of the first five years of Fresh Expressions, it is clear that the ideas in the *Mission-shaped Church* report are taking root in a deep way across the Church of England and the Methodist Church and in many other streams and traditions. There are now thousands of fresh expressions of church that are a blessing to their communities. The movement to establish fresh expressions of church seems to me to be a movement of God and part of the renewal of the Church in mission.

But the same question has stayed with me on the long miles on cross-country trains, on motorways, in coffee shops and airport lounges. Whether we are part of traditional congregations or fresh expressions: what does it mean to be church in the twenty-first century? What shapes our vision for life together today and tomorrow? What are we called to be and to do? And where will we find the strength to fulfil that calling? The questions seem to be exactly the same whether you are the dean of a great cathedral or a pioneer growing a fresh expression of church in a soft play centre.

After one trip to talk about fresh expressions of church to a conference in Germany, I came back late at night through Stansted Airport. I was pulled to one side by a customs officer and asked about my business. I explained as best I could that I was a clergyman, that I didn't have a parish and that I worked for the Archbishop of Canterbury. The man looked increasingly sceptical. 'Could you prove any of this?' he asked. All I could produce was a scruffy copy of the email inviting me to the conference in Germany. The man pondered. Finally, he said: 'I will let you into the country if you can name the Synoptic Gospels'. 'Matthew, Mark and Luke', I replied and was allowed to pass, wondering at the quality of education we give to our customs officers.

But as the journey continued I also realized more and more deeply that the customs man had pointed me to the answer to the questions I was asking about the Church. The Christian community finds its identity, its character, its calling and its strength from the person who is revealed in the Gospels: Jesus Christ.

The film *Jerry Maguire* (1996) begins with the lead character, writing a mission statement in the middle of the night. Maguire is a sports agent. For some years he has had a growing discontent with the way his business works to maximize profit at the expense of clients. The unhappiness builds, until one night at the company's national conference he writes a short paper in 25 pages with the title: 'The Things We Think But Do Not Say'. By morning there is a bound copy of this manifesto for the company in the pigeonhole of every one of his colleagues. It pleads for a return to the values of relationships and respecting people at the heart of the industry: less clients and therefore less profit. Maguire comes down the next morning to a round of applause from his colleagues. Two weeks later he is fired. The rest of the film tells the compelling story of his attempt to begin his own business again from these first principles.

This book is a kind of Jerry Maguire memo for the Church in the twenty-first century. It's written with deep love and respect for the Church. It is written to explain and explore some very deep convictions about the Church in the present and the future.

1. We are navigating through a time of great change and to navigate well we need to rediscover Jesus Christ as the compass and centre of the Church's life.

2. We need as a Church to reflect the character of Jesus to our society. But what does this mean? This is so vital we take two chapters to explore it.

3. We are called as a Church to do what Jesus did: to build up the Christian community and to change the world. It is neither one nor the other but both.

4. We will only have the strength to change ourselves or others if we are deeply rooted in Jesus. But how should that happen?

Although I am ordained, I am not writing primarily for ministers. I am hoping that this will be a book that any Christian will be able to read and talk about with friends. Although I am an Anglican, I am not writing only for other Anglicans. Here and there you will find some specific references to Anglican strengths or weaknesses but feel free to substitute your own. Although I am British, I am not writing only for the context in the United Kingdom. The Church is facing similar questions and dilemmas across much of Northern Europe and elsewhere in the world.

While I have been writing this book, God's call has come to me to begin a new part of the adventure as Bishop of Sheffield. I suspect these convictions about the Church will be tested and stretched in new ways and that I have much still to learn as my own journey continues. May God's grace be with you as you engage with these ideas and seek to follow the Lord of the Church, Jesus Christ. His call is the same to every person who reads this book and to every church: 'Follow me'.

Steven Croft

1
Finding the compass

Jesus said to him: 'I am the way.' (John 14.6)

Navigation is difficult. Every time I attempt to drive through Reading or Watford I get lost. One night I tried to find my way out of London. I drove for an hour and ended up more or less exactly where I set off. One evening in Wales I took a wrong turning, went 40 miles out of my way and ended up being very late for a conference of Welsh archdeacons (something you do only once in your life).

It was at that point that I invested in a Sat Nav system. We have had our moments, my Sat Nav and I. It has a strong preference for short cuts down exceptionally narrow country lanes (especially in the dark). But on the whole I always know exactly where I am and most of the time it takes me to my destination.

The Church, too, urgently needs its aids to navigation in the present climate. Where will we look for that perspective and direction?

Everyone inside and outside the Church in Britain agrees that we face real questions. The relationship between Church and society has changed rapidly over the last hundred years or so. That change has been accelerating in the last 25 years and shows no sign of slowing down. Some of the symptoms of that changing relationship are there to see in the way our society chooses to live its life. Sundays are no longer protected days for rest and worship. The Christian voice is no longer the dominant one in the framing of our laws. Most people are far more aware than they were of other world faiths. Church attendance over most of the last century was in significant decline.

There is more recent evidence since the year 2000 that the picture is changing: the decline is slowing down overall. New patterns of church attendance are emerging, with more people attending on different days and fresh expressions of church emerging alongside traditional worship. It's possible to discover many different places and traditions where there is real growth again. Large numbers of people still claim some kind of allegiance to Christian faith in census returns and opinion polls, but many local churches struggle to keep going with small and ageing congregations and fewer ministers to go round.

A goldfish finds it very difficult to see the water in which it swims. In the same way, it is extremely difficult to understand a changing situation in which we are caught up and to read it well, with a good sense of perspective. As I have travelled the country over the last five years listening to how people read this changing situation, I have found two very different accounts being presented to me again and again of where we are and how we arrived. One focuses on failure and the other on change. I have come to the conclusion that the first is deeply flawed and the second much more hopeful.

Have we failed?

The first account says that all of this change is happening because the Christian Church in Britain has failed and is failing. We must bear the responsibility for shrinking congregations and declining influence in society.

This is the story that is told back to the Church by the media again and again. The Church is in massive decline and it is all our fault. It is also a story that the Church tells back to itself again and again with disastrous consequences. The failure story saps strength and morale from God's people. It does so in one of two ways, depending on where we lay the blame.

Blaming others

The first way is when people lay the blame on some other group within the life of the Church. It is all the fault of the senior church leaders, says one group. It is all the fault of the liberals or the catholics or the evangelicals says another. If only everyone was 'like us', then this decline would never have happened. It is because we have been too tolerant and lax, say others. It is because we have not been tolerant and loving enough, say a different group. One party argues that the decline is because our worship is not modern and accessible. Another group argue that the same decline is because our worship is too contemporary and accessible and has lost all sense of mystery.

What is the end-product of all this blame? It is, of course, to increase bitter division in the Christian community. At the very moment when the Church most needs to be united, we blame one another for the mess we are in and become further divided. Picture an army on a field of battle surrounded by an enemy who has no need to attack at all. Different sections of the army have turned their fire on one another. Hardly anyone is even aware that they are in the midst of a wider conflict at all, which profoundly affects the future of our society. The main object seems to be to point the finger and blame everyone else within the Church as effectively as possible. As we do that, it is no surprise really that the Church becomes a deeply unattractive community to those outside.

Blaming ourselves

The second route we take is, in its way, even more corrosive. If we follow this route we lay the blame for the 'failure' not on other people but on ourselves. The decline is because we ourselves are at fault in some way. We have not loved enough, preached well enough, prayed long enough, organized effectively enough, worked hard enough to have prevailed and seen off the minor difficulties the Church faced in the twentieth century. If we had been as faithful as our ancestors, Britain would still be a deeply Christian country and our churches would all be full on Sundays.

Here the focus is entirely on our own efforts. How foolish we are. When the disciples are caught in the storm on Lake Galilee no one argues that their failure caused the wind or the rain. They do not waste time and energy blaming one another for poor weather forecasting. To have done this would have sapped strength and energy when they needed it most. They do what they can from their own resources to fight the storm, and when it proves too much they turn to exactly the person we need to turn to in our present tempests: the one who is sleeping in the boat.

When we blame ourselves, the acid of despair takes hold in the heart of the Church. At the very moment when the Church most needs the strength of Christian hope and assurance of God's grace and love, we find in our hearts nothing but despair. Our eyes turn away from God and the world and turn inwards. Despair and cynicism sap strength for new life and growth and the possibility of new things.

One of the most powerful images in Tolkien's *The Lord of the Rings* is the picture of Theoden, King of Rohan, when we first meet him. His strength has been sapped by the lies of his servant, Wormtongue, who is an agent of the evil wizard Saruman. Wormtongue's half-truths have fed the despair in the heart of the once mighty king and convinced him he can no longer lift his sword in battle and that he is powerless against the forces around him. All he can do is retrench and retreat. There are those who offer similar counsels to God's people today.

Is the failure narrative true or false?

The failure narrative has been swallowed whole by much of the Church. Either someone else is to blame or we blame ourselves. It affects ministers, church members and those who plan at local, regional and national level. But is the failure narrative the right interpretation of the present context? Where should our starting point be?

When I first became a vicar I was 29 and very wet behind the ears (some would say signs of dampness remain). One of the Readers in the church, Ken, was a Christian of great experience. Ken took me in hand like a sergeant major with an officer fresh from cadet school. One of the best things he ever taught me was what he called the 'fruit test'. Jesus says that one of the tests we need to apply to everything is the fruit test:

'You will know them by their fruits. Are grapes gathered from thorns, or figs from thistles? In the same way every good tree bears good fruit, but the bad tree bears bad fruit.' (Matthew 7.16-17)

One of the great saints, Ignatius Loyola, developed a similar principle for discerning God's will but it lacks the catchy title. Put bluntly, the failure narrative fails the fruit test. What are its fruits? They are blame and division, cynicism and despair. These are not fruits of the Holy Spirit or the signs of God's handiwork. But there are other reasons also why we should reject it.

The failure story depends on something of a myth of a golden age in British Christianity in earlier generations from which we have fallen. That myth simply does not stand up to historical examination. In every period in Church history when we look closely there are good things to find and also bad things to discover. At the time of the greatest excesses of the medieval papacy we find the simplicity of Francis. When the Church is all dry formality, God raises up Whitfield and Wesley. Christian witness and church life have always been something of a struggle since the Acts of the Apostles and the Church has always been imperfect. For every Peter and John there is an Ananias and a Simon the Magician.

This is not to deny the truth that many measures of Christian allegiance have been in decline or that our situation is serious – simply to explode as fiction that there was once a time when things were perfect. There was no golden age.

The failure story also makes us close our eyes to the very good things happening in the Church in the present. We are blind to them because these good things do not fit the script that everything is in decline and going to the dogs and it's all our (or someone else's) fault. I've often felt when talking with some people about all the good things happening in fresh expressions of church that some groups will not take them on board. New growth and new hope in the British Church simply can't happen (according to their worldview). The story of the established Church in particular has to be a tragedy with a bad ending despite the evidence of their

eyes and ears. It's more important to their own identity to preserve
the frame of this tragic story than to recognize the truth of growth
and renewal before their very eyes. Eeyore is alive and well in many
congregations, synods and pressure groups. In the last of the Narnia
stories, C. S. Lewis paints a compelling picture of a group of
dwarves who are admitted to the great banquet at the end of time
but they can neither see nor taste the good things because of their
own cynicism and despair. It's not hard to find similar groups in the
councils of the Church. But they need to be challenged.

But the main and final reason why I do not believe the failure story
is that it is simply much too *Church-centred*. We have lived in the
last hundred years through massive change in our society, which
has embraced two world wars, a seismic shift in Europe's place in
the world order, immense technological change, economic shifts
that still surprise us, political change and counterchange,
philosophical and cultural revolutions. The Church has been part
of all of this change but it has not been a leading instrument. It is
these different levels of change in the culture that have led to the
immense shifts in the relationship between Church and society. To
argue that the Church is primarily to blame for this shift is, quite
simply, to give the Church too important a place in the scheme of
things. Like the disciples we find ourselves in a storm. It would be
foolish indeed to see that storm as caused by our own actions.

As I read the Scriptures, the people of God are often caught up in
immense cultural changes. They have to respond to them, but they
do not cause them. The prophet Samuel at the end of his life found
himself in a settled pattern of ministry, judging Israel on an annual
circuit and maintaining order. But he, like us, lived in a time when
the world was changing rapidly. There were huge people
movements caused by migration. There was great technological
change as iron replaced bronze. There was economic change in the
great empires to the north and south of Israel. There was religious
and moral change as all of these other changes threatened Israel's
way of life.

God's people had to respond to these massive changes, but they
did not cause them. 1 Samuel 8 tells the story of Israel's request for
a king, for a different pattern of society and governance that would

enable the nation to survive and flourish in this changing context. Samuel is uncertain about the request at first. He is inclined to blame others and to blame himself. But his final position is to accept that change is indeed necessary and to devote the remainder of his ministry to bring it about.

Navigating change

The failure narrative itself fails the fruit test, the test of history, the test of present reality and the test of Scripture. Much more convincing and wholesome for me is the narrative that says the Church, like the rest of society, is living through times of immense change. We can only understand this change in part as yet. This change has affected every single part of our society and culture and that includes the Christian Church and the relationship between Church and society.

Does the change narrative pass the fruit test? The idea that we are navigating change produces much better fruit. People searching for a way forward tend to draw together as a community in the midst of a bewildering environment. Our focus is finding a way to progress rather than apportioning blame in the past. We are, therefore, open to help from others and generally willing to explore the past and the present, the Scriptures and the Christian tradition. We can look back to the story of God's people in the Scriptures and find many stories of journeys and moments of change in which new direction was needed. We can look back in Christian history and discover similar moments of change. Perhaps most of all, in times of change, we are encouraged to look deeper to the very core of our faith to find inspiration and a path to move on.

Discovering the compass

I believe that the sense of being lost in a strange landscape fits the present situation of the Church much better than the narrative of failure, which produces only blame and despair. Many others think so too. But if we think we are lost, that means we have to pay careful attention to how we find a path.

When I was learning how to be a Scout and walk the Yorkshire Dales I was taught how to use two vital pieces of equipment. The first was a map. The Ordnance Survey series we used was detailed, tried and tested and in clear weather with lots of landmarks it was easy to find our way. But if the fog closed in or we were on the moors without landmarks or we were simply unsure where we were, the second piece of equipment was much more vital. When we were having trouble finding the way, it was the compass rather than the map that was essential.

In this present moment for the Church we lack the precision of a satellite navigation system. We have only the sketchiest of maps. We are blazing a trail in the new territory of a global post-Christian culture. No Christian and no Church has been this way before us. But we do have a compass: a means of navigating forward creatively, constructively and fruitfully at local level, in a diocese or district or in the Church nationally. It is a compass we can all own whatever our tradition or emphasis or history.

The compass and the content of our vision for the Church is Jesus Christ. In times of uncertainty and confusion, if we navigate by this compass we are likely to stay on course. In so far as the Church reflects the nature and priorities and values and character of Jesus Christ, then we will be on course whatever the changes around us. In so far as we do not, we will be drifting away and losing our vision and direction. It is Jesus who gives the Church its DNA, its genetic code. While the Church may need to take a variety of shapes as our culture changes, it will be on course providing we discern that the risen Christ is at the centre.

This may sound a very simple and obvious thing to say. But it is worth pausing to reflect on the rock-solid biblical foundation for this idea. As I read the New Testament the idea of the Christian Church is absolutely inseparable from the person and the work of Christ. We are baptized into Christ, members of the Body of Christ and together we form the Bride of Christ. We are branches of the true vine, which is Jesus Christ, and part of the flock of which Christ is the good shepherd and for which he gave his life. We are fed and shaped in the Eucharist by the body and blood of our Lord. We are called like the disciples to live in a rhythm of being with

Jesus in community and being sent out. We are called to live and proclaim the good news of Jesus Christ after the manner and the pattern of the Son of God until that same Christ returns as king.

Whatever our tradition, flavour, party or denomination, all Christians agree that the Church is the Body of Christ and needs to be centred upon Christ. Knowing Jesus and being centred on Christ will lead us inevitably deeper into the fellowship of God the Father and the life of the Holy Spirit and into a richer understanding of the Trinity. But our starting point for the Church and our compass must be Jesus.

A mission-shaped Church is not enough

For several decades now the Church in Britain has been gradually rediscovering what it means to share in and be shaped by God's mission to our own culture and society. A kind of sketch map has emerged for the next part of the journey. We need to continue to grow traditional churches that welcome children and adults into faith and bless their communities. We need to plant many fresh expressions of church in all kinds of places and networks to reach those who cannot connect with traditional congregations and to bless different parts of our society. Since 2004, the Church of England and the Methodist Church have been seeking intentionally to grow a mixed economy Church: flourishing fresh expressions of church alongside flourishing traditional congregations. There is a short section at the very back of the book that gives an introduction to these terms (see pp. 81–82).

The desire to set the mission of God right at the heart of the life of the Church is absolutely right. But there are many questions it still doesn't answer. We may all acknowledge that we will serve our society best by developing a mixed economy of fresh expressions of church and traditional churches. But even if we agree on that question (and most of us do), we then have to go deeper and ask the next question: but how precisely are these churches of all kinds to be shaped? How are we to build their life? How are we to guide them forward? What is our dream – our vision – for God's Church in the midst of all of this change?

In this respect, the vicar of a traditional parish faces exactly the same question as a youth leader creating church in a skate park or the leader of a café church for young adults or church in a secondary school. The question is this. I am trying to grow and form a Christian community – a church. But what template am I working to? What pattern is in my head? What image do I have in my mind? What vision inspires my work? Unless I have that picture clear in my mind how can I form this community for the future?

One of the most profound effects of rapid change on clergy and congregations is that it takes away our default models for answering that key question of vision. Our default model is the recent past. What is our vision for the Church? To keep something going as we have known it from 10 years ago or 20 years ago or in our childhood or as we think it was in the nineteenth century? Change knocks away that model, that default answer, and makes us dig deeper and ask the question of vision again. There can, in the end, be only one answer to the question: what is the Church called to become? That answer is 'more like Jesus'.

As I come to the end of this five-year period of travelling across the country I have been lost many times. But my vision for the Church has grown clearer. My prayer is that over the next 20 years we will become even more than mission shaped. To be mission shaped is vital and it is essential that we learn those lessons fully. But they only take us so far. My hope is that we will find our compass again and be shaped by and take on the character of Jesus Christ in our communities. It is being centred on this vision that will, I think, give us the capacity not only to navigate through the next two decades but to flourish and be fruitful within them.

The vision to be shaped around the character of Christ is a vision that can be pursued by a small group of Christians meeting in an upper room, by a parish church, by a mixed economy deanery in its mission and by a diocese in its pursuit of discipleship.

Back to the disciples, in danger of drowning in Lake Galilee – they don't waste time and energy blaming one another; they do what they can from their own resources, but in the end that isn't enough. At that point and only at that point they turn their attention to Jesus. Isn't it time for us to do the same?

For reflection and discussion

Is the idea of the Church navigating change a more fruitful way of seeing the present situation, or do you want to hold on to the failure story? If so, why?

Do you agree that a sketch map for the Church is emerging around growing a mixed economy Church?

If the Church is meant to be like Jesus, where would you begin to explore what that might mean in practice?

2
Becoming like Jesus together (1)

> It was in Antioch that the disciples were first called
> 'Christians'. (Acts 11.26)

We often speak of communities or public institutions having a
character. Their character is a shared ethos and nature, shaped by
their self-understanding and their history and context, and which
in turn shape subsequent generations. We speak sometimes of an
institution of being demanding, volatile or anxious – at other times
an institution might be described as having its tail up, feeling
positive, being a good, stable place to be.

I have discovered that dioceses each have a particular ethos and
character. Every time I visit one diocese, at least three people come
up to me and repeat the old joke about this particular diocese
being the Dead See. It's not actually like that at all. It's a diocese
with many points of life. But that joke is a deep part of the people's
character and self-understanding. Another sees its permanent
identity as 'old fashioned' or 'low', and so is closed to new ideas.

Just like a person, a local church or Christian community has a
certain character formed by its experiences and history. A church
that has known acute suffering or shared in the suffering of its
community would bear that experience in different ways in its
character. In the middle period of my time as Warden of Cranmer
Hall, the life of the college was marked by a series of sudden and
tragic deaths. The experience of grieving together and daily worship
in the context of such suffering grew a particular character of
tenderness and gentleness in the college in those years. People
were good at looking out for one another. In a similar way, a church
that has known nothing but prosperity will be marked by that
experience. The seven short and sharp letters to different churches
at the beginning of the Book of Revelation catch seven different
'characters' in the image of the angel of each church.

But what is the character of the Church as a whole and of each local community meant to be like? I want to argue in this and the next chapter that the Church is called to be a community that reflects the character and nature of Jesus Christ to our wider society. To bear the name of Christ is also to attempt to bear the nature of Christ. The idea of a 'name' in the Bible is a big idea and implies a character as well. This is a challenging and demanding calling. When Jesus says 'Follow me!' to each disciple and to the Church as a whole, he means first and foremost 'Become like me'.

But what would that mean in practice? What would a cell group or a congregation or a circuit or a diocese (or the Church nationally) have to look like to reflect the character of Christ? We need to do some Bible study at this point.

There are many places we might explore in the Gospels to discover the character of Christ. It's an inexhaustible theme. However, the place I want to begin is the eight short statements at the head of the Sermon on the Mount, which we call the beatitudes. What would happen if we attempted to set these key verses at the heart of our vision for the Church?

The beatitudes in brief

Matthew's Gospel, as you may know, groups the teaching of Jesus into five collections, which are sometimes compared to the five books of Moses (the first five books of the Old Testament). The first and the most important of these five collections is the Sermon on the Mount in Matthew 5 to 7. The Sermon on the Mount begins with these eight balanced and short statements. We call them the beatitudes because they all begin with the word 'blessed' (some English translations also use the term 'happy'). These eight statements are to Jesus' teaching in Matthew what the Ten Commandments are to Moses. They form a beautiful and attractive description of Christian character.

In their original setting in the Gospel, they are addressed to a particular community: the first disciples of Jesus (Matthew 5.1). The term 'disciple' is a key one for this Gospel: it is Matthew who refers most to the disciples and has the Great Commission as the last words of the Gospel with the command to 'Go therefore and make disciples of all nations' (Matthew 28.19). The disciples are, for Matthew above all, the prototype for the Christian community, the Church, and named as such in Matthew 18.17 (the only references to the term 'Church' in the four Gospels).

The first time we meet the term 'disciple' in the Gospel is at the beginning of the Sermon on the Mount: before Matthew tells us what disciples are to do, we need to learn what they are called to be. What is to be the character of the new Christian community?

Each of the beatitudes is in the plural form, not the singular. It's an obvious point, but one we miss very easily today for this passage and for much of the rest of the New Testament. The sayings are primarily about not about how I am as an individual, but how we are as a group: our character together. When we read the text today we tend to go straight to the individual interpretation: this is how I am to be and to behave. But actually the eight sayings are primarily about how Christians are *together*. They are values for community living. No human being other than Jesus will ever be able to reflect all eight of these beautiful attitudes: these hallmarks of a Christian character. But, as Church, we may be able to reflect them as different Christians bring different gifts and perspectives. By and large they are not, in any case, virtues that you can practise on your own. We will learn them in community as we meet with people who reflect these qualities in different ways and as we come face to face with our own shortcomings and strengths.

The beatitudes are also all statements of hope – each one is followed by a promise. You can only seek to reshape the Church positively in the perspective of resurrection hope. Hope in the Christian tradition is not a vaguely positive feeling but a great theological virtue: a hallmark of character. Christians are called to practise hope every day, just as we are called to practise love and faith. You simply cannot reshape and renew God's Church if your starting point is cynicism or despair or ambition for yourself.

The beatitudes are also all powerful statements of affirmation. Jesus does not shape the Church in this text by criticizing his disciples, but by loving them and seeking to affirm them and to build them up in certain virtues that they already reveal in part.

Finally, taken together, the beatitudes are, I think, intended by Matthew as a summary statement of the character of Jesus himself. Matthew will go on to describe the actions and the life of Jesus in great depth and detail, and his Gospel will demonstrate to us that Jesus is all of these things. You can trace the way he does this in any good commentary or simply by reading the Gospel through from beginning to end with the beatitudes in front of you. These eight sayings capture the character of Jesus in a very concise way. I want to suggest that this is to be our vision in our formation of Christian communities for the twenty-first century. This is our compass for the guiding and guarding of the Church. This is how we are to find direction and navigate through times of great change.

As we read them through and explore them, each of us needs to try to apply them to the communities we are called to serve and shape and be part of. If you are part of a fresh expression of church, how can you help that community to reflect this character of Christ? If you worship in three rural congregations, how can they grow to reflect these virtues? If you are part of the deanery synod or a circuit steward, how can your deanery or circuit be more Christ-like in these ways? If you are responsible in some way for the diocese, then how can this be a diocese that reflects the character and person of Jesus whatever the changing circumstances of the next decades?

We believe as Christians that the risen Jesus, who has this same character today, is with us in our individual prayer and reading, as I write these words and you reflect on them, as we gather together with others in his name. One of the key ways the presence of Jesus will be shown is by the presence of these beautiful qualities in the life of his community. As we demonstrate this character of Jesus in our life together – always imperfectly – so the Christian faith is likely to become more attractive to the society we are called to serve. We need more and more to be Christians and churches with attitude: and the attitudes are to be the characteristics of Jesus.

'Blessed are the poor in spirit, for theirs is the kingdom of heaven.' (Matthew 5.3)

The first quality is, I think, genuinely the most important to Matthew. 'Poor in spirit' is an intriguing phrase. Of all the translations, I like best the one that says: 'Happy are those who know their need of God.' It's less poetic than the original, but captures the meaning very well.

Jesus is saying 'Blessed are those who know they are spiritually poor and impoverished. They are in the right place.'

Think for a moment what that means. When we know we need God then we are truly blessed. When we are self-sufficient and full of our own goodness then we are in real trouble.

Despite all the problems we face, and despite progress in many areas, the Church in Britain still does not seem to me at the moment to know in a very deep way that we are poor in spirit and in need of God's grace. We more easily, I think, convey an impression carried over from previous generations that we are rich, that we have prospered, that we need nothing (Revelation 3.17).

There are, of course, exceptions to this. But in general terms, to visit many of our meetings, you would not think that we know we are spiritually poor and dependent in every moment on God's grace. The burden of our history has inflated our sense of self-importance and self-sufficiency. We think we can get by without God.

Yet, in reality, in much of the Church in Britain we are worse than bankrupt in terms of our knowledge of God. There is no space for Jesus in many of our meetings. Why? Because we believe we can manage quite well ourselves. Our programmes for renewal all too easily turn into empty managerialism driven by budgets, not by grace and vision. As clergy, we convey to one another in our ministers' meetings and fraternals that we are doing well and have all we need. Individually, we are more comfortable boasting than we are asking for help.

Every year when I worked in a theological college I would quote the survey that was done in the 1990s on ministerial life. It revealed that the average minister worked around 60 hours per week. More than 22 hours of the total were spent in administration. Just 38 minutes per week were spent in prayer. That's less than 6 minutes per day. If that is not a definition of spiritual poverty then I do not know what is. Of all the things I have said to students over the years, that is the one that has been most often quoted back to me and clearly remembered.

There is clear evidence of a spiritual search and spiritual hunger among some sections of our population outside the Churches. Many people are looking for God in deep ways to answer real questions and hunger in their lives. The language of spirituality has for some time been creeping back into the commercial life of advertising and product labels. Some years ago, I saw a billboard that had the words 'Inner Peace!' in massive white cloudy lettering against a blue sky. It was only when I looked more closely that I saw the tag line in smaller print: 'Is having your boiler serviced by British Gas'.

But here is the strange irony. As the spiritual searching around us grows, hardly anyone associates that spiritual search with the Church. We have somehow projected a vision to our society that we are about everything but relating to God. The Church can be the most unspiritual place in the modern world, the place where it is hardest to name the name of Jesus and to admit my need of God.

My dream and vision for the Church in Britain in 20 years' time (better still, in two years' time or even the day after tomorrow) begins here. It is that we would know our spiritual poverty. I long for us to become more like the tax collector (knowing our need) than the Pharisee we resemble at present: full of our own achievements and self-sufficiency in relation to God. I hope that this might be reflected in our prayer lives and in our meetings and in our planning and in our attitudes to those around us, and that we would be known as a Church that is humble before God and not one that is self-sufficient: a Church of spiritual seekers not those who have arrived. Such a Church will be authentic and attractive to the world around us. The BBC TV programme *The Monastery* and its sequel *The Monastery Revisited* (transmitted in 2005 and 2006) showed us a religious community that knew itself to be in need of God: poor in spirit. It was like water on dry ground and had an immense effect.

As I have travelled across the Church I have found a marked difference in terms of how much time is given to prayer at official meetings. Sometimes it is not there at all. How can that happen? Sometimes it is well prepared. But it is nearly always brief and it is rarely either penitent or passionate. Why should this be so? Do we think we can do this church thing by ourselves? Are we able to navigate the immense changes we face on our own? Can we bless our society from our own resources? Do we not need God's grace every moment in every community we are part of?

One of the things that is deeply attractive to me about the people working in fresh expressions of church as I have come to know them is that they genuinely have this poverty of spirit. What the pioneers are doing often arises out of the healthy admission that something isn't working. Fresh expressions of church are needed because the existing churches cannot connect with the whole population. They know and understand that nothing can be accomplished without Jesus. They are in the place of risk and adventure and of surprising fruitfulness. This is exactly the place – on a journey of mission – that we are taken beyond ourselves and we can recapture our need for the living God.

I worked many years ago in the Wakefield diocese with a group of clergy in a deanery. Our task was to identify a focus for mission in the deanery for the coming two years where the diocese could introduce some additional resources and hope for growth and change. Most of the other deaneries found it relatively easy to identify an area of housing or work among young people as their mission priority. But this particular deanery were really stuck and the more they talked together the more difficult the problem seemed. Then, at the end of a series of meetings, one of them put into words what the others immediately said they were feeling: that the mission priority for that deanery at that time was the clergy themselves. They needed help, renewal, time, fellowship, retraining, passion in order to lead their communities through this time of change. It was a moment of becoming poor in spirit together.

And straight away they were part of the kingdom of heaven: open to grace and to growth. Our planning focused on a programme of day retreats and renewal to help them move forward.

'Blessed are those who mourn, for they will be comforted.' (Matthew 5.4)

The second beatitude is not, of course, a saying for the bereaved but, like all the others, it is a description of the character of Christ and the character of the Church. Jesus weeps often. He weeps for Lazarus his friend and for the great city of Jerusalem destined for suffering. His guts are twisted in compassion for each sick and dying person he encounters in this weary world, for the bereaved, for those cast out of human society.

As the community of Jesus we have to learn to weep. We must share the suffering of others and be a people of lament as well as of rejoicing. To live in a world where there is so much suffering must mean compassion and sorrow and tears for the grief and sorrow and pain of this world.

If we are people of compassion, how can we live in the world and not be aware of its pain – the pain caused by war and displacement, the pain of hunger and want, of needless disease or that which can be cured but is not, the pain of human cruelty and violence, the suffering that seems to have no explanation? How can we be people of compassion and not be those who mourn?

The task of the Church is not primarily to justify these events but to know about them, to bear witness, to stand in them with those who suffer, to exercise compassion and solidarity and to act as a focus for prayer. The pace of modern life, apart from anything else, often means that the cries of those who suffer are not heard. The Christian community must live slowly enough and care-fully enough to weep with those who weep.

Here it is the historic, traditional Churches that do better and the younger emerging Churches that, by and large, need to listen. The Church of England, with its sister Churches, offers an outstanding ministry in times of suffering and bereavement to countless individuals thanks to the dedication of its lay and ordained ministers. That ministry is visible in the public tragedies that strike individuals and communities, but it is exercised quietly and secretly week in and week out among the sick and the bereaved, in hospitals and prisons, and in lonely places. I found one of the most difficult and privileged parts of being a curate and vicar was taking funeral services several times a week year after year – often in tragic and difficult circumstances. I have often prayed in a vestry before a service and wanted to be in any other job than this one. But an essential and grounding part of being a Christian minister is to be exactly present in those places of sorrow and suffering and need and to carry the tenderness that grows in those places into the rest of life and ministry.

The ministry of praying for the needs of the world with compassion and faith in the heart of our public worship is a way in which we remember to mourn even in the midst of joy and celebration.

This capacity to mourn is fed and nurtured by many streams, but particularly in the Anglican tradition by the setting of the psalms at the heart of our daily prayers with their wonderful and powerful blending of lament and praise, of penitence and passion, of life's major and minor keys. To recite the psalms each day and to set them at the heart of our prayers is to be reminded in many different places that we are as a community poor in spirit. Our hearts are reminded of the greatness and goodness and majesty of God and we are encouraged to magnify our maker: to make God, not our own selves, great in our understanding:

> For great is the Lord, and greatly to be praised;
> he is to be revered above all gods. (Psalm 96.4)

At the same time we are given words to express our need of God's grace as hunger and thirst:

> O God, you are my God, I seek you,
> my soul thirsts for you;
> my flesh faints for you,
> as in a dry and weary land where there is no water.
> (Psalm 63.1)

As we read the Book of Psalms through from beginning to end, we are given words to express the deepest emotions and grief of the human heart in the psalms of lament: anguish and desolation, doubt and anger, fear and jealousy, guilt and sorrow. The psalms of lament grow our capacity to understand and articulate the sorrow and the pain of the world around us: to become people who mourn:

> My heart is in anguish within me,
> the terrors of death have fallen upon me.
> Fear and trembling come upon me,
> and horror overwhelms me. (Psalm 55.4-5)

This is a capacity and a part of our tradition that I cherish, that I want to affirm, that I want to protect as we strive to engage and re-engage with our culture. Over the last 20 years there have been many good and healthy changes to our worship, but I regret deeply the loss of the psalms from the ordinary experience of Anglican Sunday worship. In stormy water, a boat on a lake needs its keel more than its rudder or sails. The regular use of the psalms in prayer and worship is the way the Church grows a spiritual keel: able to soar in praise but weep in compassion.

This is one area where those who are beginning new forms of church need desperately to remain connected to and held within the wider body of Christ. Mission and renewal movements are often weakest in their understanding and experience of suffering. Yet without a theology of suffering – without a willingness to mourn – what begins well often ends with disillusion and defeat.

An influential book by a New Zealander, Alan Johnson, called *A Churchless Faith* (SPCK, 2002) tells the stories of people who have left evangelical, Pentecostal and charismatic churches but who have not, by and large, abandoned Christian belief. The congregations these people are part of have not, by and large, enabled their Christian faith to grow and mature beyond an initial enthusiasm and commitment. One of the reasons seems clearly to be the absence of a theology of suffering as part of the Christian life that is reflected in ordinary Sunday worship.

A temptation for the Church in times of uncertainty is that we present the Christian life as the perfect answer to every question in the hope of making it therefore more attractive to those outside. All of the difficulties, unresolved questions and human suffering are airbrushed out in our neat demonstration of how Jesus meets every human need. We need to take great care here. When people come to faith after that kind of presentation of the Gospel, sooner or later they will encounter suffering, questions and difficulties that cannot easily be resolved. What resources have we given them for these questions?

The Early Church took a very different approach. At the end of Acts 14 is a short summary passage, which summarizes the teaching and expectations Paul and his companions gave to their Gentile converts:

> They strengthened the souls of the disciples and encouraged them to continue in the faith, saying, 'It is through many persecutions [literally, trials] that we must enter the kingdom of God.' (Acts 14.22)

We need to remain and to become a Church that has the compassion and the capacity to mourn, that is able to acknowledge and stand with the pain of the world but that can hold that pain within the overall perspective of the coming kingdom of God, the defeat of death and the compassion and comfort of God's kingdom. This is not an easy calling.

'Blessed are the meek, for they will inherit the earth.' (Matthew 5.5)

I long to see a Church that is publicly known as meek and humble, that is not self-aggrandising, that is known to be more willing to serve than to be served, that gives away power and influence rather than hoards it to itself.

That is a key challenge for an established Church that, because of its history, easily thinks of itself as being at the centre of society even if, because of social change, we are now called to be for a time also at ease at the margins, on the edge of our culture. In some ways in the present moment the Church of England still inhabits the centre ground of our culture and needs to do so with a gentle confidence. In other ways we are also called now to discover God's grace and presence on the very edge of society, at the margins. Combining these two callings is demanding. We need to be on the edge because that place too is where God is found and is at work and we need to be on the margins with the same gentle confidence and hope as we inhabit the centre. Moving to the edge is a difficult and challenging experience for individuals and for churches. Our instinctive reaction is to call attention to ourselves – to demonstrate our worth, our wealth, our capacity, our wisdom – to justify our existence. It is often the insecure person who talks the most or the loudest at any gathering and who tries to draw attention in their direction. In the same way, as the Church becomes more anxious because of changes in our society, it is tempting to become more strident, to speak of how good and how relevant we are, to hold on to our position. That does not seem to be the way of Christ in the Gospels.

I think we must learn again this characteristic of meekness, which may not always be at the heart of our Church's public character but which is exemplified so well in much of our tradition. In the deeper story of the Church of England are people like George Herbert, the sixteenth-century poet and priest who stepped away from the public spotlight to invest himself in a country parish, and Edward King, the saintly nineteenth-century Bishop of Lincoln whose meekness still helps shape the parishes of Lincolnshire. In the present day, the whole world takes notice of Mother Teresa, who was meek enough to devote her life to those dying on the streets of Calcutta. Are our churches producing saints of this quality today?

I think we must learn meekness in our conversation with other faith communities in these islands and across the world. We must learn it in our openness to wisdom and knowledge from a range of discourses. I think we must learn it in our dialogue with other Christian traditions, for as Anglicans we have much to learn from Roman Catholics, from Methodists, from the black-led Churches and the new Churches (just as they may have something to learn from our own tradition). I think we Anglicans must learn it above all in our dialogues within our complex traditions and with one another as catholics and evangelicals, liberals and charismatics. We must learn it in the relationship between traditional churches and fresh expressions of church: each preferring the other if we can.

The Church in Britain at the present time is called to conduct a number of debates around what have become controversial issues. Most of these issues have arisen from our changing context. There is no doubt in my mind that we need to have these debates (although, curiously, people sometimes behave as if even to raise issues should be out of bounds). However, we are also called to have these intense and difficult debates not in private but in the public domain. One of the particular (and hopeful) features of our times is that the British population still seem to care very deeply about the future direction of the Church in these lands. The media reporting is therefore often intense and detailed. This places a particular responsibility on all involved to embrace meekness as the starting point for debate and discussion. Without the tempering of meekness, any passionately held view comes across as strident and harsh in public debate.

Meekness is not the same as weakness of character. The Hebrew language has a special word for meek, *'anaw* (pronounced, I was once told, by making a noise rather like a camel being sick). It is only used once in the Old Testament to describe an individual, in Numbers 12.3 where we read:

> Now the man Moses was very humble, more so than
> anyone else on the face of the earth.

Moses was meek but not, by any stretch of the imagination, weak. It is possible, though difficult, to combine meekness with deeply held convictions. Our model is Jesus himself.

Augustine of Hippo was a bishop in North Africa as the world changed and the Roman Empire crumbled. In his day he had the task of helping the Church navigate through a great transition. He, too, found refuge in meekness. I found these words in one of his sermons:

Construct no other way for yourself of grasping and
holding the truth than the way constructed by Him who,
as God, saw how faltering were our steps. This way is
first, humility, second, humility, third humility. And
however often you should ask me, I would say the same,
not because there are no other precepts to be explained,
but if humility does not precede and accompany and
follow every good work we do, and if it is not set before
us to look upon, and beside us to lean upon, and behind
us to fence us in, pride will wrest from our hand any
good we do while we are in the very act of taking
pleasure in it. (Augustine, Sermon 61.4)

We need to grow a Church that is meek at local, diocesan and
national level because we are the Church of Jesus Christ and this
is the character of Jesus Christ.

I think this means that there is no place for rigid divisions of
hierarchy. I think it means that we do away with some of the false
deference that abounds in the Christian community and that is
found in very formal settings like cathedrals and also in less formal
Christian gatherings and streams that have their own more subtle
rankings and deference. I think it means we may need to rethink
some of our costumes and processions in profound ways to exalt
the humble and put down the mighty from their seats (Luke 1.52).
We are disciples together before God before we are lay or ordained,
Readers or pastoral assistants, and we will be disciples together in
heaven where these distinctions will finally be forgotten.

'Blessed are those who hunger and thirst for righteousness, for they will be filled.' (Matthew 5.6)

It is the character of Christ to long for righteousness and therefore
this must be the character of Christ's Church. If you hunger and
thirst for something then you cannot help but work to bring it
about. You are incomplete and dissatisfied until it is accomplished.

Matthew's concept of righteousness has many layers. It embraces,
of course, individual righteousness before God. At one level, Jesus

is saying that when we long to be put right with God with all our heart, we will be satisfied: we find forgiveness and an end to our sense of being separated from God through the death and resurrection of Jesus.

But righteousness is, of course, much broader. It is social righteousness – justice – the values of the kingdom of God. The phrase 'the kingdom of God' in the Gospels (or 'kingdom of heaven' in Matthew) is a shorthand to describe the reign of God over creation when all injustice and wrong will be set right. Jesus' disciples are called to pray for the coming of God's kingdom in the Lord's Prayer (Matthew 6.10). We are called also to put our best energies at the service of the kingdom.

To become a disciple is not simply about being set right with God individually, receiving the gift of eternal life and then waiting for heaven. It is about devoting ourselves to the service of others and to working for a just and wholesome society. It is about keeping the perspective of the kingdom and reign of God in our common life and especially in our understanding of God's mission.

This means that in our work of telling the good news of Jesus and seeing people come to faith that we are concerned about more than the filling of pews or the making of converts. We are about seeing maturity of discipleship and lives enlisted in the whole-time service of the kingdom of God. It means that our vision of discipleship has to be much wider than that of turning up and giving regularly and doing things in church, but must embrace the whole of life and most kinds of work and service. It means we must learn to be a generous Church, giving the gifts and talents of our people in the service of others, and it means, I think, that we must learn to travel light in terms of our own structures. And it means that whenever we gather together we are mindful of the needs of others.

Note the sense of passion called for in these words. To be hungry and thirsty is to be uncomfortable in a deep way. To live in this world as a Christian is to embrace that permanent discomfort with the way things are and to be willing to spend our energy seeking justice for those who need it.

We are only part way through this exploration of the beatitudes, but already we have four qualities that form the character of Jesus himself and that are meant to form the character of the body of Jesus on earth, the Church. Like lettering through rock, these qualities are meant to be hallmarks of the Church that bears the name and nature of Christ. Like the master we follow, we are called to be poor in spirit, to be people who mourn for the suffering of creation, to be people who are meek before one another, and to be those who hunger and thirst for righteousness. A Church that sought to live and express these qualities in its common life would be a demanding but rich community to be part of: the kind of community others would want to work with and to join.

For reflection and discussion

How would you describe the 'character' of your local church? In what ways is it most like Jesus?

Which of the four characteristics described in this chapter are strongest in your local congregation? How can you affirm and encourage growth in this area?

Which of these four characteristics are the weakest? How can you encourage growth and development here?

3
Becoming like Jesus together (2)

Has Christ been divided? (1 Corinthians 1.13)

What kind of churches will flourish in the twenty-first century? I don't think myself that it will be about whether or not your building is made of stone, or whether you sing the latest worship songs or use traditional liturgy, or wear robes or not, or read the latest books or go to the right conferences. I think it will be about character: what's going on inside your community.

When Samuel has to find a new king for Israel, God leads him to the sons of Jesse, and in a famous passage all but one is brought before him. Each looks strong and capable and attractive to Samuel. But none of the seven will do. Eventually Samuel has to ask Jesse whether there might be still another son, and David is summoned from the fields. 'This is the one', God says. 'Anoint this one.' His aside to Samuel when the first son is passed over is worth remembering: 'For people look at outward appearances. But the Lord looks at the heart.'

It's a matter of character. What character needs to be at the heart of every Christian community? The character of Jesus because we are Jesus' people. In the New Testament period no one knew what to call the followers of the new sect in Judaism. Various names are recorded, including followers of 'The Way' (meaning, of course, 'The Way of Jesus'). But the name that stuck is the one that we use still today. It was in Antioch that the disciples were first called 'Christians': Christ-like people, Christ's people.

Body and Bride of Christ

The Church is hardly ever referred to in the New Testament without some reference to Jesus Christ. Nowhere is this relationship more clearly expressed than in the great images of the Church used through the Gospels and the Epistles. The two best known stress the close association between the Church as the community of believers in earth and heaven and the risen Lord. The image of the Body of Christ is particularly common in Paul's letters. The picture is used to stress the essential unity of the Church on the one hand and the need for diversity on the other: different parts of the body need to exercise different functions and ministries for the benefit of the whole.

But underlying the language of one body is this extremely close association between the risen Lord and his visible body on earth: the Church. We are not just a body. We are the Body of Christ. As this language is developed in Ephesians and Colossians, Jesus himself is described as the head of the body: it is his life, his leadership, his character that are to flow through and be demonstrated in every part:

> We must grow up in every way into him who is the head, into Christ, from whom the whole body, joined and knit together by every ligament with which it is equipped, as each part is working properly, promotes the body's growth in building itself up in love. (Ephesians 4.15-16)

If we are the Body of Christ, then it is reasonable to expect that body to demonstrate and grow into the character of Jesus himself. The same closeness and intimacy between Christ and the Church is seen in the second great image, also used in Ephesians, of that of the Church as the Bride of Christ:

> Husbands, love your wives, just as Christ loved the church and gave himself up for her, in order to make her holy by cleansing her with the washing of water by the word, so as to present the church to himself in splendour, without a spot or wrinkle or anything of the kind – yes, so that she may be holy and without blemish. (Ephesians 5.25-27)

Paul is more concerned in this passage to teach us something about the relationship between Christ and the Church than he is to give instructions about marriage. The striking, tender picture of the Church as the Bride of Christ is a direct development of the image in the Old Testament prophets of God wooing the nation of Israel as a bride in the wilderness. It expresses great passion and intimacy, both in the present and in eternity. There are references in Jesus' parables to the coming of the kingdom represented by a wedding feast or banquet (Matthew 22.1-13 and 25.1-13). The image is taken up in the Book of Revelation in the great picture of the marriage feast of the Lamb (Revelation 19.7-9).

A common feature of all these pictures is that the Church is called as the Bride of Christ to be holy: without spot or wrinkle. Although that holiness will be complete only in eternity, we are to strive for it now. What does it mean? Perhaps we need to lay on one side some of our notions of holiness, which may be about being set apart and standing back from the needs of the world, keeping ourselves pure in that sense. We need to embrace again the notion of holiness in the life of the Church being like Jesus first and foremost by seeking his character as reflected in the Gospels and, for our purposes, in the beatitudes in Matthew's Gospel. Now back to the beatitudes and the second group of four sayings.

'Blessed are the merciful, for they will receive mercy.' (Matthew 5.7)

The world we live in is not full of mercy. Relationships are sometimes marked by cruelty or indifference in words or actions rather than by undeserved, constant love. The worlds of politics, of the arts, of the workplace, of the playground are not, in general, worlds where people find mercy extended to them. Imagine the influence and the good that can be done by communities that are known to be full of constant, steadfast mercy to the needy world around them and that teach their members by example how to be people of mercy.

Yet so often it is absent. It is possible to imagine a Christian community that knows its need of God and in which you can find evidence of poverty of spirit, that mourns for the pain and sin in creation, that is meek and humble before others, and is hungry and thirsty for righteousness, and yet still lacks something essential in reflecting the character of Jesus Christ.

This missing element would be mercy. Mercy is one of many names in the Bible for the defining Christian quality of love. In particular, it is the love we do not deserve and have not earned: the faithful, unshakable covenant love of God. It is this mercy that characterizes the life and ministry of Jesus and that is meant to characterize the life of his Church. As Paul writes in his great exposition of Christian love, it is possible to practise many gifts and virtues but without love, they are worth nothing (1 Corinthians 13.1-3).

Most people in our world experience love as a kind of contract. We give our love, our friendship and our kindness to someone so that they love us back. We send cards, invite people round for meals, look out for them at work, or do them favours all in a kind of contract relationship. Often the reverse applies as well. We are sorely tempted to not speak to people, to cross them off the Christmas list, to make life difficult for them in the workplace in return for any slight or ill favour.

Becoming a Christian and becoming part of the body of Christ, the Church, means that we begin a lifelong and often difficult process of learning. On the one hand, we begin a lifetime's journey of discovering that God is indeed merciful to us, slow to anger and rich in love. He loves us before we ever begin to love him. He demonstrates his love for us faithfully and continually, whether or not we return it. That love is constant through rain and shine, through times when we return it and times when we do not. We have indeed received mercy: undeserved and constant love. We find that mercy difficult to understand because it may be unlike any other love we have ever known. At different stages of our life's journey we will need to return again and again to the foundational truth that God is merciful to us in his very nature. His love cannot be earned – only received.

But the second part of our learning, summarized in this beatitude and elsewhere in the Sermon on the Mount, is that Jesus calls us now to show this kind of love ourselves to other people inside the Christian community and outside it. This is what it means to be merciful and to be a Church that is full of mercy.

> 'You have heard that it was said, "You shall love your neighbour and hate your enemy." '

(in other words, the kind of contract love we learn in all our relationships)

> 'But I say to you, Love your enemies and pray for those who persecute you, so that you may be children of your Father in heaven; for he makes his sun rise on the evil and on the good and sends rain on the righteous and on the unrighteous. For if you love those who love you what reward do you have?' (Matthew 5.43-46)

We are to practise this kind of mercy not just in our individual lives but in the life of the community of the Church. That means that the Church Council is called to be merciful in its decision making: to demonstrate this constant, respectful love for others in all that we do together. We are to be known not only by the fairness of our dealings but by the gentleness and mercy that sometimes goes beyond fairness to communicate love.

To be a community of mercy means to be a community that tries not to judge others yet so often churches become exactly the opposite. Too often, sadly, churches are communities that love to pass judgement rather than forbearing to judge in the name of love. We assess others constantly in the inner courtroom of our hearts. We judge others very readily in our conversation for their style of dress or the way their children behave, for the misfortunes that befall them. We pass judgement especially on those who may be different from us before ever we get to know them. I've had many conversations over the years with mums struggling with bringing young children to church. It is clear that whenever their toddler makes a noise they feel that they are being judged. To use an accurate but horrible phrase I learned recently from a vicar, they are tut-tutted away from Sunday worship.

Passing judgement bolsters our own identity and insecurity, but for a Christian community it is a dangerous habit to develop:

> 'Do not judge, so that you may not be judged. For with the judgement you make you will be judged, and the measure you give will be the measure you get. Why do you see the speck in your neighbour's eye but do not notice the log in your own eye?' (Matthew 7.1-3)

Far too often local churches can be very difficult to join because, people fear, to enter a particular community is to be judged by a demanding standard. Those who come as visitors will quickly pick up whether your church is a place of mercy or of judgement. The evidence will be there in the way people speak to each other over coffee, in the notices, in the asides the minister makes during the sermon, in the kind of person who feels at home. A community that is full of mercy has the gift and grace of God to love the stranger and get to know them, to welcome and befriend without judgement and to persevere in love until mercy is returned. I once knew a man who walked his dog past the church every Sunday morning for about two years before he had the courage even to cross the threshold. His greatest need when he eventually came in was to find mercy.

I have long believed that the chief limitation on the growth of any particular Christian community is not the number of people in the area who are interested in the Christian faith. In most places in Britain, that kind of interest remains reasonably high. It is the willingness of the particular church to welcome others in, not to the occasional church service but to the real life of the community. In all the research the Church of England has done into *Back to Church Sunday*, one truth stands out above the others: when someone looks to join a church community, people are not looking for friendliness but to make friends. The initial welcome and a warm greeting on the door are, of course, important. But they are wasted if a few weeks later the newcomer has not yet formed the beginnings of a real relationship.

The quality of befriending others on the edge of community is not, of course, about learning particular techniques or adopting programmes. It is not even primarily about having healthy structures of community such as small groups or larger clusters so people can find their way in (though these are sensible and absolutely necessary beyond a group of forty or so people). Whether or not a Church community grows is primarily about the quality of mercy, of undeserved love, freely given. It is, in other words, again a matter of character not technique.

Some of the research carried out in church congregations suggests that smaller churches in particular develop people called 'gatekeepers' who act informally on behalf of the community and 'vet' potential new members very carefully through engaging them in conversation. If people pass the test (usually because they are 'people like us' or not a threat) then they are gradually introduced to others and have the chance to form friendships. But if they are not found to be suitable then there are no introductions but only cold shoulders. I found it difficult to believe that this kind of behaviour really happens because if you are the vicar of a church (or a visiting preacher) then, of course, people are almost always very pleasant and polite. It was sobering some years ago to attempt to join a church in a new place where no one knew who I was to discover that one of the key lay people in the church was incredibly rude to me for several Sundays in a row, aiming to discourage me from joining.

Not judging is one outworking of the quality of mercy. The second is to be ready to forgive. The Christian community is, by definition, a company of people who recognize that they are forgiven sinners. Such a community should, of course, be marked by and known for its readiness to extend that forgiveness and mercy to others.

Later in Matthew's Gospel it is Peter who comes to Jesus with the very specific question about how forgiving we need to be within the life of the Church.

> 'Lord, if another member of the church sins against me, how often should I forgive? As many as seven times?' (Matthew 18.21)

Peter clearly thinks he is being immensely generous at this point. After all, in the wider world people might be prepared to forgive one another once or twice. Seven would clearly be beyond all limits for society around us.

Jesus said to him, 'Not seven times.'

If Jesus paused at that point perhaps Peter and the disciples would have sighed with relief. That's all right then. He's going to say perhaps three or four times is enough. But, of course, Jesus continues:

'Not seven times, but, I tell you, seventy-seven times.' (Matthew 18.22)

A number so large you will have lost count.

The parable that follows emphasizes that it's a question of perspective. The Church is, by definition, the community of the forgiven. As long as we are mindful of how much God has forgiven us, it will not be difficult to be merciful to one another and, indeed, to those outside the community. In so far as we forget and choose to ignore God's grace and forgiveness in our own lives, our hearts begin to harden towards others very rapidly.

The Church is called to be a community of mercy that forgives easily and often. That applies to small groups of Christians, congregations and larger gatherings. A community of mercy is demanding to be part of, but also deeply attractive to those outside it.

You may have noticed by now that there is paradox in the beatitudes. There are some things that do not sit too easily together here. This beatitude on mercy is sandwiched between the call to be hungry and thirsty for righteousness and the call to be pure in heart. The Church is called to preach and to proclaim the highest standards of personal conduct and holiness of life, yet to do so in a way that is rich in compassion and mercy. Only one life has ever been lived that has expressed each part of this paradox and every other one in the beatitudes: the life that is described in the Gospels.

This is why the Church must set the study and pattern of Jesus at the heart of its reflections and will need to continually grow and rebalance its life as we neglect first one and then another of the aspects of Jesus' character.

Like many other Christians, I have pondered for many years the story told in John's Gospel about the woman caught in adultery. Those who bring her before Jesus symbolize the demands for righteousness and purity in the community. The woman herself symbolizes the need for mercy and forgiveness. Jesus is able in his own person and character not to surrender the call to purity and personal righteousness but to set this in the context of a richer and deeper mercy. If you were watching that scene enacted today, where would you stand: with the woman or with the Pharisees? And where would your church feel most comfortable?

'Blessed are the pure in heart, for they will see God.' (Matthew 5.8)

Here we are offered something that is vital in the whole matter of navigating in difficult times: we are promised that we will see God – the gift of discernment. If we are pure in heart – not as individuals but as a community – we will see God. What does this mean?

We most readily think, perhaps, of seeing God in the future when we pass through death and encounter the risen Christ in a new way. 'For they will see God' becomes a promise of an eventual reward for being good (or pure in heart). Certainly there is this layer of meaning, but there are others.

'Seeing God' does not need to wait until we are with the Lord. It can begin here. To be pure in heart may mean, perhaps, being able to discern God more clearly in holy things: when we are caught up in worship, as we receive communion, as we meet in fellowship with other Christians and as we read the Scriptures. There is something of this kind of seeing in the story of the two disciples on the road to Emmaus. For much of the journey they cannot see who is walking with them. It is only quite late in the evening when they eventually recognize Jesus in the breaking of the bread.

But I believe the promise is wider still. God is present in particular ways in fellowship, Scripture and sacraments. But these are not the only ways we discern his presence. If as a community we are pure in heart, says Jesus, we will be able to see where God is at work already in the lives of those around us and we will be led to join in. This discernment will shape our mission as a Church and our calling as individuals. If we are pure in heart, we will be able to see God, perhaps, even in difficult and traumatic periods of our lives, in times of pain and suffering, and discern ways forward. If we are pure in heart as a Christian Church, even in these times of immense change in the twenty-first century, we may be able to see God in all of this change and find the good path.

But what does it mean to be pure in heart? Like all the other qualities in the beatitudes, the term has a rich background in Scripture and carries two distinct meanings. The first is being inwardly clean or holy. Jesus makes it clear later in Matthew's Gospel that the natural condition of a human being is to be unclean within. In a major dispute with the Pharisees, Jesus teaches his disciples that it is not what goes into us that defiles us but what comes out of the heart – the centre of our being:

> 'For out of the heart come evil intentions, murder, adultery, fornication, theft, false witness, slander. These are what defile a person, but to eat with unwashed hands does not defile.' (Matthew 15.19-20)

The Church in our day has rather lost confidence in talking about holiness and purity of heart and life. It's possible to see why. It is difficult in our present context to talk about purity of heart and life without sounding like the Pharisees themselves. As soon as we take hold of this beatitude it is as if we let go of mercy. But we cannot let go of this call to inner purity either. As Jesus goes on to make clear in the Sermon on the Mount, the implications of the gospel challenge not only our outer actions but our words, our inner thoughts and our motivation. The strictest standards of his day condemned murder. Jesus sets the standard of purity as insulting someone else. The standards of his day condemned the act of adultery. Jesus sets the standard of purity as looking at another person with lust. The standards of his day condemned breaking a solemn oath. Jesus sets the standard of purity at being people of our word all the time (Matthew 5.21-37).

How can we realistically strive after this kind of purity? We need to rediscover the central Christian truth that we become pure in heart as Christian people not by pulling ourselves up by our own bootstraps or keeping sets of rules, but by living in, and being transformed by, God's grace and God's Holy Spirit. The Spirit is so consistently called Holy because the Spirit's work to transform our lives, to cleanse us from within, brings out fruits (or qualities) that, again, are the very qualities of Jesus:

> The fruit of the Spirit is love, joy, peace, patience, kindness, generosity, faithfulness, gentleness, and self-control. (Galatians 5.22-23)

The Church is called to be a community where lives are changed and where people learn to live well. We are to create communities where people keep their word and their promises, where men and women are set free from the sexualization of relationships, where we do not insult or dismiss one another with cruel words, which distort lives. Through Scripture and sacrament, through shared lives and the Spirit's gentle work, there should be a steady growth in grace and goodness. That process will be more intense and measurable during the early years of a person's Christian journey as there is a putting right and remaking in the image of Christ, and particular teaching and support will be needed. However, that steady growth in holiness will be something that for all of us continues until we are with the Lord. Community life in the Christian Church needs to be deep enough and real enough such that we encounter one another and encourage one another in this journey. Who would not want to join a community where, through God's grace and the support of others, we learn to be more loving, more patient, more joyful and better able to control and direct our lives from within?

In different places, I see both traditional churches and fresh expressions of church taking steps in this direction. Wherever local churches take seriously teaching about how to be married or to bring up children, how to live a balanced life, how to manage your finances, they are making strong steps forward. All too often though, we concentrate only on the churchy bit of living. In church Sunday by Sunday we teach about how much to give to the local church but not about debt and budgeting; we teach about how to pray but not how to grow in hope or joy.

There is a second meaning to the phrase 'pure in heart', which has at its root the notion of being single-minded in devotion to God, not distracted by other passions and concerns. Jesus' words in the Sermon on the Mount about not being able to serve two masters echo this idea (Matthew 6.24). But the concept is caught best in Scripture in the challenge of the prophet Elijah to the people of Israel when he summons them to Mount Carmel. At the time the Israelites were divided: some following the God of Israel and others following Baal, but most hedging their bets and adopting a pick-and-mix approach to their religion. Elijah challenges this attitude very deeply, asking:

> 'How long will you go limping with two different opinions? If the Lord is God, follow him; but if Baal, then follow him.' (1 Kings 18.21)

The confrontation on Carmel that follows is designed to force the issue and engender purity of heart.

As the Christian Church navigates through this time of immense cultural change in Britain today, we will need the quality of meekness towards other views, faiths and opinions, but we will need to match this with a deep and single-minded devotion to God, Father, Son and Holy Spirit. Again there is a paradox, like a man or woman walking along a ridge with valleys on either side. On the one side is the valley where meekness overbalances into the Church being so accommodating that it loses all distinctiveness. If being a Christian is so like everything else then what is the point? On the other is the valley where the Church becomes so distinctive it completely loses touch with the surrounding culture. It is absolutely impossible to frame a set of rules for every Christian and situation that allows us to navigate well. The way forward is in developing a character in the Church as a whole that reflects the character of Christ.

'Blessed are the peacemakers, for they will be called children of God.' (Matthew 5.9)

Please note that Jesus does not say: 'Blessed are those who avoid conflict, for they will be called children of God.' Nor does he say: 'Blessed are those who are nice' or even 'those who are peaceful'. He says: 'Blessed are the peacemakers.' Conflict is normal. We need to get used to it.

Conflict is an inevitable part of Jesus' ministry in the Gospels. He rebukes the Pharisees and other Jewish leaders. He overturns the tables of the money changers in the Temple. He confronts the disciples. He rides into Jerusalem as king, directly challenging the rule of the Roman Empire. He promises not peace, but a sword (Matthew 10.34).

As we read the rest of the New Testament, conflict also seems to be an inevitable part of establishing healthy Christian communities in an uncertain situation. Things have to be worked out from first principles, and there are different points of view on all kinds of areas, from where to buy meat, to how to wear your hair, to how to worship together, to how to handle personal relationships.

If Jesus and the Early Church experienced this kind of conflict in a time of mission, uncertainty and change, then we need to take heart. The conflict we experience in the Church today often makes us feel uncomfortable. However, perhaps we should see conflict not as exceptional in the life of the Church but normal and normative, especially in periods of mission and change.

Every period of Church history suggests that conflict is normal for the Christian community. But if that is the case, then gifts of conflict resolution – or peacemaking – become absolutely vital and especially in times of change. One of the difficulties of our present situation is that, many of us, being English, tend to find conflict temperamentally very difficult. We try if we can to avoid conflict, or to pretend it's not there, or we imagine that it can be overcome with 'niceness'. But it is simple reality that every church in a mission situation faces difficult decisions and we will sometimes disagree about them. Every traditional church in a time of change will face a degree of conflict about what to do about a range of different issues. Every fresh expression of church that is gathering a community of people from a different culture and calling them to lifelong discipleship will also face question after question, and the answers are not always easy or self-evident. We simply cannot navigate through change as a local community or as a church without embracing conflict and the tools of peacemaking. The alternative to the path of conflict and peacemaking is the path of a Christianity that offends no one (which, of course, is not real Christianity at all).

I find conflict and peacemaking uncomfortable, and my first instinct in any conflict situation is always to either avoid it or smother it with niceness. A very good colleague and friend of mine once wrote a sketch about the team we both worked in, assigning each person to a character in *Winnie the Pooh*. I got to be Pooh – the bear of very little brain. Whenever Pooh was asked a difficult or controversial question in the story he would reply 'Tiddly Pom!' and walk away, humming to himself. It was a revealing moment for me.

As I read the Gospels, I do not see Jesus either avoiding conflict or smothering it. He sometimes embraces or provokes conflict for the sake of the gospel and the people he is seeking to reach with God's love. And he is never, ever, merely nice.

In our own conflict resolution we need urgently to get beyond the conventional patterns of politeness and learn instead some genuinely useful skills of peacemaking. These include listening, attention, discipline, mediation, compromise, honesty and the willingness to forgive. We certainly need our specialists in this area: those who have a particular vocation to be peacemakers. However, in a mission context, as many have argued, these gifts need to be part of the toolkit of every lay and ordained minister. They also need to be part of the habit and discipline of every Christian community. In Matthew 18 Jesus offers very direct and challenging instructions to the whole community to help them to be peacemakers and resolve conflict appropriately:

> 'If another member of the church sins against you, go and point out the fault when the two of you are alone.'

[note the opposite of niceness and conflict avoidance] 'If
the member listens to you, you have regained that one.
But if you are not listened to, take one or two others
along with you, so that every word may be confirmed by
the evidence of two or three witnesses . . .' (Matthew
18.15-16)

If we are to grow peacemakers, then as churches we have to learn
how to handle conflict well internally and that means it needs to be
talked about and taught about. As a vicar in a local church, from
time to time I used to receive very strongly worded letters criticizing
my own ministry or some aspect of the local church. I used to find
them so embarrassing and difficult to deal with that I would bury
them in a file somewhere, worry about them and take them out
and read them every time I was feeling down. I had to learn to
gather the confidence to show them to someone else, talk them
through and respond more appropriately. A third party is almost
always needed.

But handling internal conflict well is just the beginning. Imagine
the impact if the Church in Britain became an institution that
intentionally became so good at handling conflict that we were
able to be a powerful witness to, and support to, other groups in
society wherever conflicts arose? That pattern has been followed
in other parts of the world, most notably South Africa. But the
skills have to be learned and practised within the community of
the Church before they have credibility beyond it. If that can
happen in a divided society, then truly we will be given the highest
accolade by those around us: 'they shall be called sons and
daughters of God'. Churches may be less comfortable places
to be, but perhaps they would also be more worth investing in.

'Blessed are those who are persecuted for righteousness' sake, for theirs is the kingdom of heaven.' (Matthew 5.10)

Finally, we reach the last beatitude of the eight. (Matthew 5.11
is normally taken as a different kind of saying that expands and
explains the final short, balancing saying in verse 10.) Like the first

quality of being poor in spirit, it is extremely challenging but in
a different way. It carries exactly the same promise as the first.
Those who are poor in spirit and those who are persecuted for
righteousness sake will both inherit the kingdom of heaven.
But what does it mean?

I think that Jesus is saying that if the Church is faithful in being
a community that lives out the first seven qualities, then we will
also experience difficulty and persecution. The two go together.
Difficulty is an inescapable part of the Christian life, and some of
that difficulty will arise because those around us find the Christian
Church uncomfortable. I think that Jesus is saying here that if
we do not as a Church experience some of this difficulty and
persecution then we may not be living out these qualities: we
will have lost our saltiness (Matthew 5.13).

The strangest paradox of all in the Gospels is that the one who
came to bless, to heal, to forgive and to cleanse was himself
persecuted for righteousness' sake, arrested, whipped and
crucified. Jesus promises faithfully that to become a disciple
means to take up our own cross and to follow in his way, and
that this journey of faith will be a costly one (Matthew 16.24).

A Church that is learning again from Jesus about how to live in
a strange new world must be a Church that is prepared sometimes
to stand against the tide of a culture and society. It needs to do this
in the name of what it believes to be right, and to pay the price in
terms of persecution for the sake of righteousness. If we are not
prepared for this, then our whole journey will be one of bending
and accommodating to the culture. We will have nothing distinctive
to bring.

It is likely – though not inevitable – that in the coming decades
our society will be a less and less comfortable place to live as a
Christian. We must prepare ourselves and our fellow disciples for
that journey. For many hundreds of years in Britain, our culture and
society has been shaped generation after generation to support the
attempt of the majority of the citizens to live the Christian life. Until
a very short time ago, Sundays were legally protected for rest and

worship, as were a number of Christian festivals or holy-days. This applies now only to Christmas and Easter – and many schools have in the last few years separated their spring holiday from the Easter festival. Making the choice to be married and faithful within marriage was supported by the law, by financial advantages and by the broader culture. Religious leaders were accorded significant respect and a place of honour in society, even if that was not deserved. Some of this remains. The Christian faith continues to have a privileged place in our governance and constitution, in our education and healthcare, and most aspects of our national life, which in turn supports local churches and individual Christians as they live out their discipleship.

However, with each decade that passes, this cultural framework of support for living the Christian faith grows weaker. It is important to do what we can to resist most of these trends, for the good of society as a whole. A society that takes one day off in seven for rest and re-creation will be a better place to live for everyone than one that is driven by greed to work 24 hours a day 7 days a week. However, at the same time, as distinctively Christian communities, we need to grow more accustomed to living against the grain of much of our culture. That will mean, on the whole, that the churches – the Christian communities – will need to grow deeper and stronger to provide the necessary support to individual Christians who are living against the flow.

In so far as the Christian community is perceived as trying to live differently, then this will from time to time provoke persecution. A friend of mine when he became a Christian found that he stopped swearing at work. That was all he did. He never mentioned his faith or why his language had changed. But it was enough to provoke a strong and unpleasant reaction from his colleagues, which was hard to bear. We are not, at present, talking about violence or even legal discrimination as in many parts of the world (though there have been some interesting test cases about the right to wear a cross at work), nor are these more severe forms of persecution even remotely on the horizon. But we can clearly see the need now for the Christian Church to be intentionally different again from the society in which we are set, to march to a different drum, and that will sometimes be uncomfortable and costly.

What then is the Church called to be?

The Church locally and nationally is blessed in so far as we are community reflecting the character of Jesus Christ. There are many ways of describing what this might mean in practice, but we have explored in these chapters the eight sayings in the beatitudes that sum up both the character of Jesus and his ideal for the Church, which bears his name and which is his Body and his Bride.

The Church is blessed, in other words, when we are poor in spirit, when we mourn for the needs of the world, when we are meek, when we hunger and thirst for righteousness, when we are full of mercy, when we are pure in heart, when we are peacemakers, when we are persecuted for righteousness sake.

In this journey to become more like Jesus, we need each other. No one individual is sufficient to capture and reflect all of these qualities. In any local church and in a wider grouping there will be individuals who embody one quality or another clearly enough to catch a vision of what it might mean to hunger and thirst for righteousness or to be meek. We also need to hold on to the obvious, but often forgotten, truth that the Church as we are now is by its very nature imperfect. If we were already as Jesus intends us to be one day, then he would hardly have given us the Sermon on the Mount. Looking at how far short we fall of the ideal should not therefore drive us to despair – still less to judgement on our fellow Christians – but to a fresh commitment to shape our communities well to reflect these vital qualities.

As we engage in this re-shaping then, the Church will find in the midst of this rapidly changing world that we have a direction again, a true north by which to navigate. We will find, too, that we are blessed as Christian communities in the sense Jesus promises here. We will possess the kingdom of heaven; we will be comforted; we will inherit the earth; we will be satisfied; we will receive mercy; we will see God; we will be called children of God; we will possess the kingdom of heaven.

Much conversation about the life of the Church in a time of change, perhaps naturally enough, focuses on outward organization either to manage decline or to restructure for mission. If we are focusing on managing decline then our dialogue is focused on how to stretch the resources of ordained ministry and develop the right range of recognized lay ministries to sustain existing communities. If we are focusing on restructuring for mission, then our dialogue will be focused on how to sustain existing traditional congregations while developing the capacity for planting and sustaining fresh expressions of church.

This conversation is vital, but if it is to be effective our dialogue about the Church must go deeper still. The Church is not first and foremost a human organization, but a community called into being by Jesus and intended to reflect his character and nature. If we can focus first and foremost on growing churches that reflect the character of Christ in the beatitudes then we will find, I believe, a pathway through the most difficult of changes that lie ahead. We will become more and more like Jesus' people.

For reflection and discussion

How is the quality of mercy reflected in your small group and local congregation? What more do you need to learn?

How does your church handle conflict and how can you learn habits of peacemaking?

How do you experience the difficulty of living as a Christian in today's world? How does it feel like living against the grain of the culture?

4

Building the Church or changing the world?

Did Jesus focus in his ministry on changing the world or on building up the community of disciples? Think back to the Gospels. How do you read the stories of miracles and healings, the confrontation with the scribes and the parables? How do you read the story of Jesus' passion, death and resurrection? What is Jesus' main aim? Is it to found a community or to proclaim God's reign in the whole of creation?

The only sensible answer, of course, is 'Jesus did both of these things'. There are many places in the Gospels where Jesus' horizons are very wide and his concern is to proclaim and demonstrate God's reign in the whole of creation. There are also many places where Jesus is focused on the disciples, bidding them to come apart. The focus in these passages is on their own growth and development as the community of God's people.

As a Church we are Jesus' people. We are called to do what Jesus did. If Jesus focuses on both of these things, then the Church must do the same.

Yet here is a mystery. For much of the last 50 years in Britain, the Church has behaved as if there really was a choice to be made. Some streams and traditions have focused on building up the Church and have neglected the call to change the world. Other streams and traditions have focused on changing the world and have neglected to grow and to build up the Church.

We cannot claim to be Jesus' people unless we are doing what Jesus does. But before we explore this terrible false dichotomy in more detail, we need to ask a much more basic question.

Are we called to do anything at all?

It may be a surprise to some church members that the Church as a whole is called to do anything. It may even be a surprise to many that a Christian is called to do anything other than live in a certain way. We live in a society in which most of us are used to thinking of ourselves as consumers with wants, needs and rights in every area of our lives, but we find it much harder to grasp responsibilities.

There is a series of short films on YouTube® about *meChurch*: the Church that caters for everyone's needs without making any demands. My favourite clip is a mock television commercial that runs like this (the words in **bold** are the deep American voice-over and the words in *italics* are spoken by prospective members):

> **Imagine a church where every member is passionately, wholeheartedly and recklessly . . . calling the shots.**
>
> *What about a church that starts when I get there?*
>
> **OK. When you arrive, we begin.**
>
> *I want a pastor to come to my house to deliver the sermons.*
>
> **No problem. Expect a knock at your door within 24 hours.**
>
> *Financially, Cherie and I don't give a lot but we'd like to know who does and how much.*
>
> **Join now and you'll know what every person gives in detail.**
>
> *When I'm in the church service can my car get a buff and wax?*
>
> **Not just that but an oil change and a tune up.**
>
> *How about tickets to the superbowl?* **That's asking too much.**

I'm serious. If I'm going to join I want tickets for the big game.

Alright. You join now and we'll get you there.

I'd like a pony.

Look in your back yard.

Me Church. Where it's all about you.

We may smile at the *meChurch* films, but only because we recognize they are partly true.

As we think about belonging to a church, it is very natural to most of us to think: 'What will I receive and gain from belonging in this way?' We may look carefully at the youth work (if we have children), or the teaching, or the quality of worship, or the opportunities for fellowship and ministry. Our focus in a consumer society is much more on what we might gain than what we might have to offer and contribute.

Clearly, churches have to operate in the society in which they are set. Many churches have worked out, therefore, that in order to grow a thriving church community in twenty-first-century Britain it is absolutely necessary for the sake of the gospel to meet people where they are, and that means effectively meeting their precise and unique needs: fellowship, engaging worship, good teaching and so on. These are real needs and people don't flourish as Christians unless they are met, any more than people are not sustained physically without food, drink, sleep and exercise.

So far, so good. But it is very easy to allow this balance to move too far in the other direction, and so stress the benefits of church membership and belonging that we take away the costs and demands of the gospel.

When Jesus calls the first disciples he does not call them only to meet their own needs. Mark 3.14 is one of the earliest descriptions of the Christian Church and it remains one of the most memorable. We know that both Jesus and Mark are making a statement about the Christian Church in this passage because of the number of the disciples who are called. Twelve is not simply a random number or a conveniently sized small group. The disciples are the continuation of Israel, which from the very beginning had 12 tribes. At this founding of the Church, the people of God, what does Mark say is to be their hallmark?

> He appointed twelve, whom he also named apostles,
> to be with him, and to be sent out. (Mark 3.14)

The Church is brought into being by Jesus who calls people into this new community. The life of the Church is to be marked by a rhythm of drawing together in worship and fellowship and being sent out to share in God's mission. That rhythm of drawing together and being sent out can be seen through the whole of the Gospels as the disciples gather around Jesus and are sent out again. On several occasions in the Gospels Jesus reminds his disciples that to follow him means self-denial and sacrifice:

> 'If any want to become my followers, let them deny
> themselves and take up their cross and follow me.'
> (Matthew 16.24)

This sacrificial way and only this is the way to find life in all its fullness:

> 'For those who want to save their life will lose it, and
> those who lose their life for my sake will find it.'
> (Matthew 16.25)

This element of call and commitment can be seen in the life of the Early Church, both in Acts and the Epistles. It is vital for Christian people to come together in worship and fellowship. But it is also vital for our own life and health as Christians and for the sake of the world that we engage in God's mission (the word 'mission' means 'to be sent'). To be church is to live in this rhythm of worship, fellowship and mission: coming together and being sent.

If we do not live in this rhythm of worship, fellowship and mission then we are not church.

There is a particular danger in a time of anxiety and low confidence that we go to such lengths to make the Christian faith and Christian community attractive that we remove any sense of commitment, of obligation, of demand and difficulty from the Christian life and from Christian discipleship. We emphasize benefits but not responsibilities.

But if we proclaim only this kind of watered-down gospel of weak commitment then we are simply being unfaithful to the teaching and practice of Jesus, to the witness of the Early Church, and to the lives of the saints down the ages who have given so much and sacrificed so much so that we can receive the life-giving message of the gospel. Christianity that does not call for a faithful, committed whole life response is not Christianity.

Moreover, removing the demands from both the Christian gospel and the life of the community actually makes both much less attractive to the person who is seeking a new and different way to live.

The apostle Paul is the greatest exponent of the grace and goodness of God and the good news that we can do nothing to earn or win God's favour. Our lives are set right with the God who made us, only because of his great love in the sending of Jesus Christ his son and through Jesus' death and resurrection. We receive these gifts through faith.

In the Letter to the Romans, Paul spends eleven whole chapters explaining and exploring this mystery of God's great gift to us. However, he does not shrink then in Romans 12 from explaining clearly what our response to that gift and grace should be: complete commitment.

> I appeal to you therefore, brothers and sisters, by the mercies of God, to present your bodies as a living sacrifice, holy and acceptable to God, which is your spiritual worship. (Romans 12.1)

The human life is meant to be lived in surrender to God's love and grace and in seeking God's will. A community of people who are jointly seeking to live their whole lives in that way is one of the greatest gifts we can receive. Membership of the Christian Church is not simply about turning up one Sunday in three and putting some loose change in the collection plate. It is about offering our whole selves to God, to one another and in service to the world.

Many years ago I took part in a mission with a Christian mime artist whose work captured extremely well the step that many people who are part of churches as consumers need to take. A man is in church singing a hymn. The collection plate comes round. He feels in his pocket, takes out some change and puts it in the plate. He carries on singing.

A few seconds later the plate comes back. He looks up to heaven and back to the plate. Sighing, he takes out his wallet and puts in first one note, then another, then the whole wallet. He carries on singing. The plate comes back. The man writes out a long cheque. He puts in his car keys. He puts in his house keys. He carries on singing.

The plate comes back. The man looks up to heaven. He looks at the plate. He removes his jacket, his shirt, his shoes, his trousers. He carries on singing (and shivering) in the cold church.

Again the plate comes back. Again the man looks up to heaven and down at the plate. But at last the light dawns. He puts down his hymn book and climbs slowly and carefully on to the collection plate.

God is not looking for our spare time or our loose change. In the Gospels, Jesus did not call disciples who wanted merely an extra hobby or interest in their lives. This is about the whole of our life. In response to God's grace we offer our whole selves to be a living sacrifice. This, and only this, is Christianity.

A Christian Church is not a gathering of loosely committed consumers or more or less satisfied customers. It is the living community of those who are offering their whole lives to Jesus Christ and will live in this dynamic rhythm of worship, fellowship and mission: coming together to be with Jesus and being sent out in love and service to God's world. This, and only this, is what it means to be church: Jesus' people.

Whole life discipleship: a double vocation

How do we as a Church live out this dimension of being sent? Discipleship is lived out in our whole lives, not simply in one part. To be a disciple is about every part of our lives now: our work and our leisure time as well as our prayers and specific acts of Christian service. It is certainly not only, or even mainly, about that part of our lives we spend in specifically Christian activities. To be a disciple is about commitment to Christ over the whole journey of our lives from the point at which a person becomes a Christian: life as a young person, a young adult, in mid-life and through to old age. When an adult or child is baptized into Christ and into membership of the Church, then that marks a beginning of a life of dedication and commitment.

But where in that life of dedication and commitment should we as a Church focus our energy? How do we understand our mission as part of God's mission? What does it mean to be sent and to be sent together as the disciples were? In particular, how are we to balance our calling on the one hand to build up the Body of Christ, the Church, and on the other to serve and change the world?

There is no doubt according to the Scriptures that we are meant as a whole Church to engage in both of these adventures: to build up the Church and to change the world. The vision of God's purpose in the whole of Scripture is not to call a special people for himself out of the world, but to call a special people to bless the whole world.

God does not want the world to be as it is today. The Bible contains a vision of human life and living where everyone has access to security and justice, protection and shelter, the right to earn a living through work that satisfies. It is a vision where the hungry are fed, where old people live in dignity, where children are protected, where lives are not destroyed by war, where all people have purpose and meaning in their lives, and where men and women exercise responsible care of the creation.

As we have seen, the Gospels tell us that Jesus came proclaiming the kingdom of God (or, in Matthew, the kingdom of heaven). This phrase 'the kingdom of God' or 'the reign of God' is a powerful shorthand for the whole of God's vision for the world and its future. 'The kingdom of God' is code for the world as God intends it to be. That vision of the kingdom is revealed piece by piece like a wonderful jigsaw in the pages of the Old Testament and especially in the psalms and the prophets. You cannot simply turn to one chapter or a single passage and grasp it all. It takes a lifetime of studying the Scriptures for the picture to be discovered and filled out.

God's kingdom comes in a new way with the ministry of Jesus and we see in the Gospel many signs of that kingdom: the sick are healed, lepers are cleansed, children are set at the heart of the community, women are treated equally with men, the dead are raised. From the time of Jesus' ministry we have been living in the time when God's reign on earth has begun, but has not yet come in all its fullness. That is why we pray in the Lord's Prayer: 'Your kingdom come.' We pray in hope and confidence that one day the Lord will reign on earth as he reigns in heaven.

And we know that, like Jesus' first disciples, we are called to be the Church – the community that bears witness to the good news of the kingdom of God – God's vision for the world. The call of the Church is to hope for that vision to come about, to live as an (imperfect) sign of God's kingdom and to work to establish the kingdom of God on earth wherever we live.

Again, so far, so good. But let me focus the question more sharply. Much of the Church makes a choice here to put its energies in one basket or the other. Should we be concentrating on building up the life of the Church – which prays for the kingdom? If this is our priority, our energies will go into church-based activities, into evangelism and small groups and teaching missions. Or should we be putting our energies directly into improving the life of the local community, into its schools and charities or economic regeneration or serving the homeless or promoting the care of the environment?

For the Church as a whole, of course, this is a trick question. It's not either–or. It's a both–and. We are called to build the Church and we are called to try to change the world according to God's vision for creation.

But this is one of the areas where we have most lost our way. We think there is a choice to make when actually there is none. Different churches and different Christians seem to need to embrace one of these only (as if they were alternatives) and look down on those who embrace the other as second class and misguided. What happens as a consequence of this false dilemma?

Building the Church without changing the world

The first seems to be a particular danger in a period of perceived Christian decline when the Church seems to be losing its confidence in the 'reach' of the gospel. We see the need so clearly to set the priority only on building up and growing the life of the Church. Often that means, in practice, setting the priority on growing the life of our own local church. All the energy becomes focused within that community. As a consequence, we lose the broader perspective, the wider horizon of the Church in the purposes of God's kingdom and seeking to change the world. Sometimes we lose perspective deliberately and sometimes accidentally, but the consequences are the same.

This kind of thinking is very evident in church vision statements and mission statements that only express the purpose of the church in 'building the church' language. 'This church exists to make disciples' would be one example. 'Our vision is to grow the church' would be another. There are many local parishes in the Church of England now that express their goals predominantly in terms of numerical growth.

Sometimes this thinking is evident in all the energy being channelled into the life of the congregation or in the themes of the sermons. The preaching is only focused in effect on how to be a good church member and how to invite others to join. The application of every sermon can be reduced to 'Come to church more often; give more money; do more in church and bring others to evangelistic events.' The implications of the gospel for family life, for leisure, for the wider community and for working life are ignored completely.

The horizons we set in public worship set the horizons for the church community in its living. Where we emphasize growing the church in numerical terms only, the horizons for Christian faith can often shrink to this one congregation and its needs.

I had a sobering conversation a couple of years ago with a group of clergy over a meal. I was doing a bit of informal research at the time on how many churches were using the Lord's Prayer in their worship and how much. They admitted, not very much. Then one of them said something that disturbed me profoundly: 'And we never really pray for the world either.' 'Tell me more', I said. 'We don't really have time', he replied. 'We have an extended time of worship, we have a sermon and then we have a ministry time. There is no time to pray for the world.' I never asked, but I am almost sure, that both the worship and the ministry time would be focused on the life of the individual and building up the life of the congregation.

The church that ceases to pray for the world regularly has lost the horizon of the kingdom of God. There are many churches like this up and down our land. Such a church is also (incidentally) not following the teaching in the New Testament on worship (see 1 Timothy 2.1-2). I would suspect, but I can't be sure, that such a church has almost certainly stopped reading the Old Testament in its worship and especially the psalms and the prophets. They have lost the pattern of the jigsaw that is the kingdom of God and care only for the growth of the church.

And this will not be the end of the story, for there is a greater danger still around the corner. Over time, as we lose the wider horizon of God's kingdom and our call to change the world, our view of God himself becomes smaller and smaller. Little by little, God is no longer the Almighty Father, Lord of heaven and earth, creator of the universe and potentate of time who loves each part of creation. God becomes simply local: the Lord of the local congregation concerned only with our lives, our building fund, our quarrels, our projects and, eventually, our prayers for parking spaces.

When a church gets to this point, we can no longer claim to be introducing people to the whole of the Christian faith but to a small part of it. By this point, such a church will be placing an undue emphasis on the ministry of the ordained (whose main energies are indeed focused on building up the church) and neglecting the wider discipleship of the whole people of God. Such a church needs to return to the Scriptures, to widen its horizons and catch again a sense of the greatness and wonder of God and of his vision for creation. We need the perspective of God's desire to bless the whole world. We are called to do more than grow the local congregation if we are to serve the purposes of God.

Changing the world without building the Church

But if one error is to focus on building the Church without paying any attention to the wider world, then the other is equally dangerous. It is to focus on building the kingdom of God – changing the world – while paying no attention whatsoever to building and growing the life of the Church.

There have been, and are many, examples of that kind of error in the recent life of the Church of England. Once again, it is an error that arises from anxiety and despair. Building the Church is very difficult. We fear people are not interested in Christian faith and commitment. So we focus all our available energies outwards in doing good and seeking to transform society, and we neglect severely the building up of the life of the local church. Evangelism and sharing faith is caricatured and denigrated on this view as being all about 'bums on pews'. What have we come to when we use derogatory phrases to dismiss the precious task of growing and building Christ's Church?

The consequence of this opposite error is extremely serious. The Church does not grow by itself. A Christian community, like a garden, will turn to a wilderness rapidly if it is not tended. If there is no ploughing and sowing, there will be no harvest. As in a family, if care is not invested in those coming to faith – whether as young children or adults finding faith – then they will not grow to maturity. Left to itself without maintenance, the building will crumble and decay.

If the local church is not built up through the investment of time and love and creativity and passion, then it will certainly decline and that decline will be rapid. Churches grow because people invest in them. Since the time of the New Testament the Christian Church has always been one generation away from extinction. No one is born a Christian. Every single Christian needs to learn the faith and grow into it for themselves and that demands energy and effort from those who would teach them.

If you need to be convinced that this work of building the Church is vital look no further than the Gospels. There is a dangerous idea, which was taught to many clergy educated in the middle of the last century, that Jesus' only concern was the kingdom of God and not the Christian community, but this is manifestly not the case.

It is, for certain, absolutely clear that the horizons of Jesus' mission are wide. Jesus preaches about the kingdom of God. He lives out the vision of the prophets. He models the life of the kingdom. His miracles are signs of the renewal of creation and the setting right of the whole of society. He lives a mission-shaped life.

But Jesus' particular care and concern in the Gospels is to grow the community of the disciples who are the Church, the new Israel. This small community has a high purpose in that broader horizon of the kingdom of God: to be salt and light, to witness to God's grace, to make disciples who will live out and pass on that message from one generation to another, to seek to bless and change their wider world. This group are Christ's own flock and he is the shepherd; they are the branches, he is the vine. Through these branches the light and life of Christ comes into the world.

How do we build the Church? We need to invest in the basic building blocks of community life. They are very obvious, but in times of change it is the obvious things that are forgotten. Every local church is built up through word and sacrament, which, as we will see, sustains the community in its discipleship. Every local church needs to be a place of real community and care. Every local church needs to take responsibility for the care and nurture of children and young people in the Christian faith. All too often congregations, which happen not to have children present, become congregations that are unwelcoming to children. Every local church needs to provide a place where an adult can come and learn about Christian faith for the first time. Every local church needs to take seriously the call to begin fresh expressions of church for those who have no church background and need to begin from the very beginning.

Making sure these six elements are present in the life of every local church is not an impossible task. Read through the list again and check how many marks out of six you would give your own congregation. But here is the reality: so often, so very, very often, they are not there. What is more, in some contexts (thankfully not many these days) some of these things are regarded as eccentric and not for 'our kind of church'. Rebuilding is needed at a very basic level.

To build the Church in these ways is a high and holy calling and we should honour those who are called to this ministry and who invest their own lives in the life of God's people – whether they are stipendiary ministers or self-supporting. I am deeply weary of the tired dichotomies between evangelism and social action. We are called to both, and we neglect either at our peril. We need to preserve the wider horizon of the kingdom of God. But we also need to invest time and energy in building up and growing the Christian community. That building up of the Church is to be set within the wider horizon of working for the kingdom. As Christian disciples we are called to build the Church and change the world.

Gifts, calling and discernment

There is one more place we need to go to briefly in this look at what the Church is called to do. The Church as a whole needs to pay attention in its life both to building up the Church and to changing the world. Jesus pays attention to both, and so should we.

Together we have one calling. However, very early in the life of the Church, the first Christians who wrote the New Testament develop very strong concepts of different gifts being given to different members of Christ's body and different callings for each person.

Some of these gifts and callings are primarily about building the Church: the pioneer who is called to build a new congregation; the person who pours their life into teaching faith to children; the evangelist who leads an evangelism course again and again. We are to treasure and affirm people with these gifts, equip them, sustain them and honour them. Some of these gifts are about serving and blessing and changing the world: the teacher who stays in the same primary school year after year; the volunteer co-ordinator for the local hospice; the artist concerned to glorify God through music or painting. We are to treasure and affirm people with these gifts, equip them, sustain them and honour them.

Romans 12 begins by stressing that our response to God's grace is offering our whole selves back to God as a living sacrifice. But Paul goes on immediately to stress that the way in which this works out in practice for each of us will be very different. It is our natural human tendency to give some gifts and callings more honour and respect than others, but we are to resist this:

> For by the grace given to me I say to everyone among you not to think of yourself more highly than you ought to think, but to think with sober judgement, each according to the measure of faith that God has assigned. For as in one body we have many members, and not all the members have the same function, so we, who are many, are one body in Christ, and individually we are members one of another. We have gifts that differ according to the grace given to us . . . (Romans 12.3-6)

The calling to build the Church and change the world is not addressed to individuals, but to the Church as a whole. As individual people we have to work out where we fit in within that overall mission. Each of us has different gifts to offer. God does not expect the impossible from any individual. There are a wide variety of gifts described in the New Testament and they are combined in an infinite number of combinations among God's people. All gifts come from God and are given by the Spirit. Some are natural talents or skills. Some seem much more to be given directly by the Spirit who equips the Church in mission. Some are learned or enhanced through training and life experiences.

Through the course of our lives and through sharing in the life of the Christian community, one of the ways we learn where we fit in to God's mission is by discovering the particular gifts we have been given. A second way is by asking the question of where the needs are at any particular time. What most needs doing in this place at this time? The foundation of all Christian ministry is service and being ready to serve. But the third question we need to ask is, 'What is God's call to me in this season of my life?' What is my vocation?

Again, the Bible speaks clearly about God calling a wide range of individuals to a wide range of ministries both in Church and society. The idea of calling is not restricted to those called to do things in the life of the Church or to the ordained. God calls people to use their gifts in certain professions through their full-time work. God calls others to particular roles within families or communities.

Within the whole body of the Church each of us is called to discover where we are called to serve in God's mission at any particular time of our lives. We discover this through knowing our gifts, being aware of the needs around us and discerning God's particular call. Each of us will be called at any particular point in our lives to fulfil a number of different responsibilities: to look after ourselves, to lead a life that balances prayer, rest and work in a sustainable rhythm, to care for our own families, to live as Christian disciples in the workplace, to take on different roles and ministries in the Church, to serve in different capacities in the community.

All of our lives change and evolve, sometimes due to our own choices and sometimes due to circumstances beyond our control. We may deliberately move jobs or area or get married. Our children may leave home. Our own health or the health of a family member may fail. Our working life may change dramatically. Each of these major events brings a vocational junction: a chance to assess again our gifts, the need and our particular calling and to consider afresh what the balance needs to be in the next period of offering our lives back to God. Over the course of a lifetime we should expect seasons where we are resting and well as seasons of activity and fruitfulness.

In all of this, as the Church of Jesus we will seek to become more like him, seeking to grow the beautiful attitudes that were so much part of his character. And we will seek as well, like the first disciples, to be with him and to be sent out both to build the Church and to change the world.

For reflection and discussion

Do your sympathies lie with building the Church or changing the world? Have you lost one perspective or the other? If so, how can it be restored?

How wide is the horizon of worship in your church? Is it as wide as the kingdom of God? How can it be developed?

How many marks out of six would you give your local church in terms of welcome and growth (see p. 59 above). Where do you need to focus now?

What is your own personal calling at this stage of your life?

5
Finding the strength for change

'Apart from me you can do nothing.' (John 15.5)

Many Christians and many churches feel overstretched. There is always so much to do. There is always slightly too much in the programme. There are too many messages to respond to. There are too many people to see. There is a certain look that crosses the faces of many ministers when a speaker is brought in to encourage them to do more. 'I'm struggling to keep up with things as it is. How do you expect me to add more?'

How is a Christian community to find the strength generation after generation patiently to grow qualities like mercy and forgiveness and peacemaking? Where will Christians find the resources to enable them to live against the grain of our society in an increasingly demanding world? Where does the inner strength come from to attempt to serve the community or to change the world without becoming burnt out or corrupted, disillusioned or distracted? Where are we to find the capacity consistently to offer the simple building blocks we need to build the Church for the next generation for children and for adults: the children's groups, the nurture courses, the fresh expressions of church?

All of these endeavours require energy to be invested year by year over the long term. But where does it come from? Humanly speaking, I am a Christian today because almost 50 years ago my local vicar came to visit a new family who had moved into the area, because my parish church cared enough about children to offer a Sunday school where volunteers gave their time, because there was a Cub pack and Scout troop led by people who invested in young people, because the vicar cared enough to teach a confirmation class to young people, because a young mother cared enough to begin a small youth group with just three teenagers and kept at it for the next ten years, because the diocese offered events for young people where a growing faith could crystallize and so on. In adult life I went for lunch with Mr Wharton, the man who had been vicar of the parish where I grew up when I was three years old. It was a moving moment when, after lunch, he took out his old visiting book and found the records of a visit to a new family who had just moved into Daleson Close. There was my name, in an ancient notebook, a sign of care and welcome and prayer and a life invested in ministry.

But this demanding work of change cannot be sustained unless we are connected to the source of all life and strength: to the life of Christ himself flowing through the Church. We are called to be Jesus' people as we grow to be like him. We are called to be Jesus' people as we do the things that Jesus did: building the Church and changing the world. But we are called to be Jesus' people in this third way also. We are sustained in our discipleship as we spend time together with our Lord. 'He appointed twelve, whom he also named apostles, to be with him, and to be sent out' (Mark 3.14). If that connection to the life of the risen Jesus is real and sustained, then as Christians and churches we will be like the bunny in the adverts for the everlasting battery: keeping going mile after mile after mile with the same vitality.

The gospel story is marked by this rhythm of the disciples gathering around the Lord to be refreshed, renewed and sustained and then being sent out again to engage with the world around them. All four Gospels bear witness to the promises of the risen Jesus to continue to be with the disciples, both as they gather together and as the go out in mission. This rhythm was not intended simply for Jesus' ministry before the resurrection, but is meant to be part of the experience of the Church in every generation. It is the heartbeat of the Christian life. We need now to unpack and explore this idea of the life of the Church being sustained by the risen Jesus. What does it mean? And how does it work in practice?

The vine and the branches

In John's Gospel, Jesus develops our understanding of the life of
the Church through a series of vivid images, all of which connect
with themes elsewhere in the Gospel and all of which connect the
Christian community with Jesus himself. Most are contained in a
series of seven sayings beginning with the words 'I am'. The first
and the last of these simple and powerful images are about how
disciples are sustained and find strength as they live the Christian
life together. It is no accident that the two images Jesus uses
connect us to Holy Communion.

In the first of these seven sayings in John 6, Jesus is the bread of
life (John 6.35). As the Israelites were sustained in their journey
through the desert by the manna that came down from heaven,
so Jesus sustains his disciples in their journey through this world.
The Church, put simply, is the community that is fed by Jesus:

> 'I am the bread of life. Whoever comes to me will never
> be hungry and whoever believes in me will never be
> thirsty.' (John 6.35)

John 15 is the central chapter of the last discourses and comes mid
way through Jesus' teaching on the gift of the Spirit. It is here that
Jesus gives us the last great image of the Gospel before we come to
the passion narrative. Jesus is the vine and we, the Church, are the
branches. It is this image that takes us further than any other in
discovering how the Church is sustained as we grow more like
Jesus and engage in God's mission. In essence, finding strength for
change for a Christian is not about training or technique but deep
abiding in Christ. The words may be familiar to you but try to read
them slowly, phrase by phrase, as the words of Jesus.

> 'I am the true vine, and my Father is the vinegrower. He
> removes every branch in me that bears no fruit. Every
> branch that bears fruit he prunes to make it bear more
> fruit. You have already been cleansed by the word that
> I have spoken to you.
>
> Abide in me as I abide in you. Just as the branch cannot
> bear fruit by itself unless it abides in the vine, neither can
> you unless you abide in me.

> I am the vine, you are the branches. Those who abide in
> me and I in them bear much fruit, because apart from me
> you can do nothing.
>
> Whoever does not abide in me is thrown away like a
> branch and withers; such branches are gathered, thrown
> into the fire, and burned. If you abide in me, and my
> words abide in you, ask for whatever you wish, and it will
> be done for you. My father is glorified by this, that you
> bear much fruit and become my disciples.' (John 15.1-8)

In pride of place at the heart of the last discourses in the fourth
of the Gospels to be written down, as the last great image of the
Gospel, comes this clear and beautiful many-layered image of the
vine and the branches. It is an image of the Church in relation to
her Lord.

I love this passage for many reasons, but one of most important is
the use of the term 'fruit' to describe what should flow from the
life of the Church and the life of the disciple. The picture has deep
roots in the Old Testament. The prophet Isaiah describes the nation
of Israel as God's vineyard. He comes looking for the fruit of
righteousness and justice, but finds only sorrow and bloodshed.
The same images are picked up in the parable told in the other
Gospels about a vineyard (Mark 12.1-12) and in many other places.

What does Jesus mean by fruit? Fruit in the biblical tradition means
exactly what we have been exploring together. It means both our
character and our actions. It is neither just one nor just the other,
but both together.

As we have seen, when Paul describes the fruits of the Holy Spirit in
Galatians 5 he focuses on the development of character and a
transformed life:

> The fruit of the Spirit is love, joy, peace, patience,
> kindness, generosity, faithfulness, gentleness, and
> self-control. (Galatians 5.22-23)

But the metaphor applies equally in the Scriptures to the
transformation of society, as in the Isaiah 5 passage where the

fruit the Lord seeks is primarily social righteousness and justice. It applies also to an increase in the number of disciples: to growing the Church. In Matthew 9 Jesus uses a slightly different agricultural metaphor to describe a harvest that needs to be gathered in. This means primarily those who are going to join the Church and be part of the kingdom, rather than a harvest of character or a transformed society:

> 'The harvest is plentiful, but the labourers are few;
> therefore ask the Lord of the harvest to send out
> labourers into his harvest.' (Matthew 9.37-38)

When disciples abide in Jesus and Jesus in them, like branches in a vine, then there will be fruit in terms of changed character, growth in the Church and transformation in society. One kind of fruit cannot be separated from the others. Each depends on the connection between the branches and the vine.

Here is a strange thing. The Church, like much of the world around us, has borrowed its language of failure and success from the Industrial Revolution. We like to talk about bold visions of continuous growth, of increased output, of expanding capacity. We imagine, somehow, that these things can happen automatically. They are mechanical images. Provided we put the right systems in place or the right programmes, provided we have the right recipe and include the right ingredients, then certain results will follow in an ever upward graph of growth.

The flaw in these images is that human communities are not in the least like machines. They are idiosyncratic and unpredictable. They sometimes change because of the smallest or weakest person in them or because of a dramatic or tragic event. When a football team changes its manager its fortunes can swing dramatically, even if all the players stay the same. Morale and confidence are extremely subtle things and cannot be created by formula.

I think, myself, that this industrial language of continuous expansion and growth is damaging for most institutions: it is not healthy for a school or hospital or business to go through year after year of long-term expansion or to imagine that this is even possible. However, it seems particularly damaging when the Church borrows this industrial language of growth and imagines that any local community can sustain year after year of rapid and continuous expansion. Sooner or later the quality of the life of the community will suffer as its numbers grow.

Jesus never, ever, speaks about success or failure in the life of the Church. He talks about fruitfulness or a lack of fruit. That fruitfulness will be evident if the branch is connected to the vine. However, it might be evidenced in different ways in different communities at different times according to the community and its context in wider society. It may be seen in growth in character and the quality of discipleship. It may be seen in an increase in numbers. It may be seen in the transformation of society. It may be any combination of the above.

Jesus seems to imply that, over time, growth and fruitfulness in all these ways will be normal but that no kind of growth is meant to be continual or steady. The picture of the vine is much more gentle and sustainable than the language of growth drawn from factories and big business. The fruitfulness we are to see in the branches of the vine will be seasonal. It is likely that, in God's economy, seasons of bearing fruit in the life of any local church will alternate with seasons of being pruned and cut back. A season of expansion may need one of consolidation. Jesus even says that it is precisely when we are fruitful that we will experience this sense of then being pruned so that this particular branch may be even more fruitful. A season of growth in numbers in a local congregation may need, in God's husbandry, to be followed by a season of consolidation as those new Christians learn to be more like Jesus and like the community they have joined, and become in turn a blessing to the society around them.

So, like our Lord, we should be both generous and gentle when we look for fruit. It may be there in different ways, and it may not be there all the time. Seeing fruit will sometimes be a process of discernment. But Jesus is also clear that, over time, we should be able to see significant fruit in any local Christian community – in any branch of the vine – providing that branch is rooted in Jesus and remains in him. If we cannot see that fruit at all over several 'seasons', then there is something badly wrong. The language of the image shows that this, too, is entirely possible and to be expected. Not every branch does in fact bear fruit. The only conclusion is that the branch is not abiding in the vine and surgery will be needed.

According to Jesus himself, the source and the secret of lasting fruitfulness for any Christian community is not technique or good planning or the latest ideas. It does not rest primarily in great leadership or wealth or natural human ability. It does not depend on the context in which we are set. The source and secret of lasting fruitfulness is whether or not we are connected to and abiding in the vine: it depends on our connection to Jesus. If we are not living and abiding here, then no amount of strategy can bring fruit from a dead branch. If we are connected, then no amount of clumsy leadership can prevent some fruit appearing. Sadly, there are many churches in the country that are not well led. But within them it is possible to find the saints of God who are abiding in the vine, which is Jesus, and are bearing fruit in acts of mercy, in peacemaking, in keeping hope alive, in living out their faith in the workplace and in blessing their communities.

If the branch is rooted in the vine, then the life of the vine flows through the branch to produce fruit, much fruit that will last. If Christian disciples and their local community, the church, are rooted in Jesus, then the life of Jesus will flow through their lives and the fruit will be seen in characters that reflect the character of Jesus, in the gathering in of the harvest and the building of the life of the local church in numbers, and in blessing and transforming society around:

> 'Those who abide in me and I in them bear much fruit.'
> (John 15.5)

So what does this mean in practical terms for Christian disciples and their local community to be rooted in Jesus as branches are rooted in the vine?

Four pathways

What are the ways God has given to the Church to stay rooted in the vine and so bear fruit? It should be no surprise to us that different Christians at different times have found different combinations of ways of staying connected and finding the strength for change. But growing to be like Jesus and doing what Jesus did are not negotiable for any church. We should expect variety, but also some common elements.

The most convenient and often quoted summary is in Luke's first description of the life of the Church after Pentecost. Following Peter's sermon, we read, about three thousand were added to the Christian community. This is fruitfulness indeed in terms of growth in numbers, but a time of consolidation is now needed. How is this community to be discipled and rooted in the risen Christ? Luke tells us in the very next verse:

> They devoted themselves to the apostles' teaching and
> fellowship, to the breaking of bread and the prayers.
> (Acts 2.42)

Acts 2.42 is quite often quoted on its own as a church mission statement or vision statement. This is a very serious mistake. On its own, Acts 2.42 is completely inadequate for this purpose. There is nothing in the verse at all about sharing in God's mission to the whole of creation and there is nothing, for that matter, about Jesus or reflecting the character of Jesus in the world. It may sound a little harsh, but a Church that spent all its time in these four activities would not actually be a Church at all: it would be entirely focused on its inner life and not on bearing fruit in and for God's world.

What Acts 2.42 does give us though is a very concise, memorable and authoritative statement of the four ways or habits we need if as a church and individuals we are to remain rooted in Jesus the vine. Our situation is different from the disciples of Jesus' day. We cannot seek him out on the shores of Galilee after a demanding period of mission and activity. But we can find him in the ways and means God has appointed for the Church in every generation: in the teaching of the apostles, in fellowship, in the breaking of bread and in the prayers.

The phrase translated 'they devoted themselves to' is worth pausing to reflect on. Luke is not describing here a single event on the day after Pentecost, nor is he talking about a particular season in the life of the Church. The sense is continuous over time and carries the meaning of 'persisting in' or 'holding fast to' or 'keeping going in'. We are talking here about building strong and persistent habits or disciplines in the life of the community to ensure that we abide in Jesus and that our life is rooted in the life of God. If we want to see renewal in many traditional congregations, then these disciplines need to be recovered and made more central. Empty practices or stale habits need to be reinvigorated with life. If we want to see strong and sustainable fresh expressions of church, then these disciplines and habits need to be taught and learned. There will be no consistent Christian growth and fruit without them because these are the ways that the Church learns to live in Jesus.

The wisdom to grow in these shaping habits is often contained in the deep traditions of church life: the very traditions that can be dismissed or left behind as the Church struggles to make itself more relevant. The discipline of reading the whole of Scripture is contained in the gift of following a lectionary that seems a difficult discipline for a new community to master but is a vital safeguard against error and imbalance. The discipline of remembering the Christians of the past is caught in the practice of saints' days and other festivals reminding us of those who reflected in their own lives something of the character of Jesus.

The apostles' teaching

The phrase 'the apostles' teaching' is a clear reference to the Scriptures. The teaching of the apostles according to Acts is constantly rooted in the Old Testament Scriptures. The teaching of the apostles as it was written down forms the New Testament through which Christians read and interpret the Old Testament. Reading the Scriptures is not primarily an individual activity, but something we do as a Church. More often than not in our individualized world where each of us owns several copies of the Bible, we get this the wrong way round and see Bible reading as primarily a solitary activity. When the Christian Church assembles together we read and explore the Scriptures in both Old and New Testaments. The word of God is alive and present in the community through the power of the Holy Spirit to equip, to sustain, to challenge and to bring life. The Spirit of God works through the Scriptures as they are read and expounded to bring new life and a connection to the life of Jesus, the living Word of God.

The breaking of the bread

'The breaking of the bread' is a reference to the Lord's Supper or the Eucharist. The early Christians certainly did eat together frequently and this eating together is an important expression of community. We are told this in Acts 2.46 and elsewhere. But the phrase 'the breaking of the bread' is something of a technical phrase in Luke and Acts. It is used in the Emmaus road story as the disciples recognize Jesus. It is used in several subsequent passages in Acts. Holy Communion is the meal given by Jesus through which the Church remembers his life and death and resurrection as the central gospel event, which calls the community of the Church into being. Holy Communion is the meal we eat in anticipation of the great banquet in heaven. It is here that the Church receives the bread of life, manna for the journey. It is here that we are sustained and able to abide in the vine. Some churches today are so used to the Eucharist as their main Sunday service that it has ceased to become a holy event or meeting place. There needs to be a rediscovery and a recovery of a sense of God's presence. Some fresh expressions of church (though not all) are slow to discover the powerful and converting presence of Christ in the simple action of taking, giving thanks, breaking and sharing together.

The fellowship

The Church of Jesus Christ is designed to be sustained through word and sacrament. We are sustained also through fellowship, the gift of community. This community is not about superficial nodding acquaintance but real relationships one with another. As Acts goes on to make clear, it is about the sharing of resources, about practical support and love, about care for the poor in the Christian family. It is in community that we form strong bonds of friendship and affection, where we learn from the example of others, where our rough edges are knocked off, where we see the living demonstration of meekness, hunger for justice and peacemaking. What passes for fellowship in many congregations is some way removed from the New Testament gift of common life experienced in Christ. It needs to be recovered by sharing meals together, through creating temporary communities, through mission together (in which we face outwards but work side by side), through gifts of honesty and appreciation and taking time to develop shared history. In a world that is relationally impoverished, this kind of community will be like water on dry ground.

Traditional congregations and fresh expressions of church have much to learn from each other here. Fresh expressions of church need the wisdom of the Church down the ages as they wrestle with ways of centring their new communities around the teaching of the apostles and the breaking of bread in appropriate and imaginative ways. But fresh expressions of church often grow out of new initiatives to grow community and they have much to teach traditional congregations about the value of open doors and lives and the forming of life-changing relationships at the heart of what it means to be church.

The prayers

Finally, Luke tells us, the Church in the first and every generation needed to devote itself to 'the prayers'. This is slightly more formal language than saying that we need to devote ourselves to 'prayer' in the abstract. Intercession and individual prayer are important, but the meaning is slightly wider here. Again Luke is referring to something the Church does together: the evolving rhythm of worship and common prayer, which has always been at the heart of the Christian community, sustaining its life from season to season and year to year. It embraces both daily prayer said by individuals, gathering in smaller groups for prayer and worship and the regular gathering of the church community in its assembly Sunday by Sunday in the rhythm of the Church's year.

You might think it would be normal for any Christian team or group or church to give careful and regular thought to the way in which it prays together. In reality it is surprisingly rare. The same patterns continue in home groups and staff meetings, in Sunday gatherings and midweek services year after year. Sometimes they can be life-giving, but as often they become dry and need to be refreshed. Within the Fresh Expressions team we have entrusted to one member of the team the call to help the rest of us to pray together when we meet and to pray for one another when we do not. This has meant that each time we gather (and wherever we gather) there has been careful thought and preparation – 'devotion' – to the prayers. That means in turn that the team has a sense of abiding in the vine – of staying connected to our Lord.

Fruitfulness

In the passage that follows this clear summary of how the Church is sustained and consolidates its life, Luke draws attention to the many different fruits, which flow from being rooted in God in these four distinct ways. There are many wonders and signs done by the apostles. There is a deep sharing of lives and possessions. The community have goodwill with all the people: they are a blessing to their society. 'And day by day the Lord added to their number those who were being saved' (Acts 2.47). As we read on in Acts we discover that these fruits do not happen automatically or passively: it is still essential for the Christians to go out and live out their lives engaging in the mission of God. But the life of Jesus Christ, the life of the Spirit, is flowing through this early Christian community because they are rooted securely in these ways.

The Christian Church has evolved and changed in many ways down the centuries. At the time Luke was writing, the Church was a small minority group under real threat of persecution from both the Roman Empire and from Judaism. The Church grew and bore fruit in such a way that it became the majority faith of the Roman Empire. The gospel was carried by missionaries to every part of the world and the Church was born in many different cultures. Even today the Christian Church continues to grow and expand throughout the world. During two thousand years of history Christian faith and practice has been carried in the great rivers of the East and West, through the Protestant tradition, by Pentecostalism and by many smaller streams. The ways in which Christians have met and worshipped together have varied enormously and remain varied today. We will not see in the future a more uniform Church in this respect and we would, in my view, be foolish to try and build one. But the same four elements Luke identifies in Acts 2.42 have remained central, more or less, in every stream and tradition. From year to year each Christian, each local community, each diocese or regional Church, each great communion, stays rooted in the life of the vine as we devote ourselves to the apostles' teaching and fellowship, to the breaking of bread and the prayers. These are the ways the Church of God is sustained in the life of God and for the mission of God.

Christian ministry

All Christians are called to serve God in the whole of their lives. However, since the time of the apostles, ordering the life of the Church so that together we stay connected to the life of God has been seen as a vital task. As we have seen, unless it is done well, with love and discernment, there is a real danger that the Church will become separated from her Lord and cease to bear fruit.

For that reason, from earliest times, the Church in every tradition has taken care to set aside, or ordain, ministers to care for and to nurture the life of the community, to help the Church to be with Jesus together and to be sent out.

Some of these ministers are gifted and set apart in order to help the Church to grow deeper in sharing in the life of Jesus. Their task is to pass on the teaching of the apostles, preside at the breaking of the bread, intentionally build up the fellowship and lead the community in the prayers. These ministers were called from earliest times 'presbyters' or elders in the community, the term from which we derive the English term 'priest'. The heart of their role is to help the branches to live in the vine.

Some of these ministers are gifted and set apart in order to lead the Church in its work of being sent out. From earliest times to the present the Church has set aside certain ministers primarily to be missionaries: to go out from the Christian community to share the gospel and to plant new churches. Paul and Barnabas and their companions exercise this kind of ministry in the New Testament. These ministers are called in the New Testament by the name 'evangelists' or 'deacons'.

But even this was not sufficient, because the life of the Church is more than the life of any single local congregation. A third kind of minister is needed whose role is to connect together these local congregations into one body, to lead the Church in mission to God's world, to ordain new ministers for the congregations, and to represent the churches in their interaction with the society around them.

The Early Church chose the name '*episcopos*' for this kind of minister. It means someone who watches over the life of the community. The English term 'superintendent' is a literal translation, used in the Methodist Church for the minister who watches over and leads the life of the circuit. We derive the term 'bishop' from the same Greek word: a bishop is a minister who watches over and leads the life of the Church in a diocese and ensures it abides in the vine and bears much fruit.

The apostles' teaching, the fellowship, the breaking of bread and the prayers are not an end in themselves. They are given by God as ways in which we abide in Jesus in order that we might bear fruit in changed lives, in a growing Church and in a transformed society.

In the same way, the different ministries in the life of the Church are not given as an end in themselves or because the people called to these ministries are special in some way or a different kind of Christian. They are given so that the life of the Church can be ordered in such a way that we continue to abide in Jesus and bear fruit in changed lives, in a growing Church and in a transformed society.

'Because apart from me', says Jesus, 'you can do nothing.' (John 15.5)

Abiding in the vine

It is no easy task to shape the life of a community in such a way that God's life remains central. A Church Council can easily become simply a business meeting with no prayer. A meeting of a local ministry team can become simply a committee deciding on the next service rota. A Sunday service can easily degenerate into a string of notices: more like a school assembly than a gathering of the people of God. Where this kind of thing happens, things may carry on as they were for a little while. But eventually these church communities will find, over time, that they dry out and there will be little strength to change. The road for renewal for many congregations does not lie in doing more but in reconnecting again with Jesus, the source of the Church's life: through retreat, word and sacrament, and the fellowship and the prayers.

As a Church we are called in this moment to navigate a period of real and substantial change in our society. To navigate that change well we need confidence in God's love and God's purposes. So many ills in the life of the Church spring from anxiety and fear. We also need a clear vision for the future. We are called to be people who together grow and reflect the character of Jesus in the beatitudes. We are called to be poor in spirit, mourning for the world, meek, hungry and thirsty for righteousness, merciful, pure in heart, peacemakers and so distinctive that we attract opposition. We are all called to live generous and sacrificial mission-shaped lives as disciples of Jesus seeking to do as Jesus did: building the Church and reshaping the world in the light of God's love. We find the strength for this immense and holy calling only as we as a community remain rooted in the life of the risen Jesus, becoming a channel for his grace and love in the world.

The Book of Psalms begins where we will end, with a beautiful and moving picture of the life of the righteous within the community. Psalm 1 is not speaking about individuals but about a community of God's people within the nation. The righteous 'are like trees planted by streams of water, which yield their fruit in its season, and their leaves do not wither' (Psalm 1.3).

May the life of Jesus be present always to help the Church of Jesus Christ bear fruit in changed lives and a changing world. May we together become more and more Jesus' people.

For reflection and discussion

How does your community abide in the vine?

Who are the people called to sustain the community in that abiding, to lead in mission and to oversee the life of the whole?

Are each of the four ways of abiding discussed in this chapter in place?

What might you need to do or think differently as a result of engaging with this material?

Afterword

There is, of course, much more to be said about what it means to be the Church than can be said in one short book. I have argued that to find our way through the twenty-first century we need to re-centre our life and understanding of the Church upon Jesus Christ. But that is, of course, only the beginning. Through God the Son there is much to be discovered and learned of God the Father, the creator and sustainer of the universe, and God the Holy Spirit, who breathes life into creation. Exploring the fullness of God the Trinity reflected in the life of God's people is the work of a lifetime.

In the first chapter of Ephesians, Paul writes in a powerful and moving way of the unsearchable riches of Christ. At the beginning of his prayer he affirms the Ephesian Christians who have established the right centre and starting point for their journey:

'I have heard of your faith in the Lord Jesus and your love towards all the saints' (1.15). He then builds out from that centre, praying that the Ephesians may grow in their knowledge of God, seeking to push their horizons wider and wider, opening up a breathtaking panorama of the life of the Trinity in the whole of creation. Yet, at its conclusion that panorama returns to the person of Jesus Christ filling all things and drawing all things to himself.

There is much more then to be said than can be said here. This little book is simply a beginning in re-imagining the Church as Jesus' people. There are many other lines to be explored. Yet there is no other foundation for the Church than Jesus Christ.

And finally . . .

There are many excellent and substantial books on what it means to be the Church in the twenty-first century.

However, I would point any individual or group wanting to explore the themes of this book further to the following:

The Gospel of Matthew

The Gospel of Mark

The Gospel of Luke

The Gospel of John

Fresh expressions and the mixed economy Church

In 2004 the Church of England took stock of recent developments in mission and Church planting in the ground-breaking report, *Mission-shaped Church*. The report developed new language to describe a range of ventures, which aimed to create church for those outside the Churches: fresh expressions of church. In accepting and commending the report, the Church of England as a whole blessed this new wave of missionary work in our own society. Four years later there are thousands of fresh expressions of church across the country seeking to connect with people who are outside the Churches. Some are large projects with one or more supported ministers. Most are small and local and led by existing ministers and teams of lay volunteers. The Churches have established extensive training programmes to equip the pioneers who are called to begin these new communities. There is a growing body of wisdom about good practice (www.shareheguide.org.uk). The Church of England has created a new focus of ordained ministry to lead this work and there are increasing resources flowing towards this kind of mission (for more details on all of this see www.freshexpressions.org.uk).

The Church of England, the Methodist Church and other denominations and streams increasingly see their engagement in mission within the United Kingdom as continuing to bless and serve our whole society, but with this dual focus of continuing to build up traditional congregations on the one hand (for those who have some kind of church background) and establishing fresh expressions on the other (to connect with those who have none). Together, these traditional churches and fresh expressions of church form an increasingly diverse mixed economy of church life that can serve and bless an increasingly diverse society. The language and concepts of fresh expressions of church, pioneer ministry and the mixed economy Church are being increasingly adopted as helpful by the Church in other parts of the world where the Church faces similar challenges: in Australia, New Zealand, Canada, Holland, Germany and Scandinavia and by other streams and traditions within the United Kingdom. We still have a long way to go both in terms of learning how to do this well and in seeing good practice spread across the Churches, but a good beginning has been made and the fruit is already significant both in the numbers of people we are connecting with and healthy developments in Church and society.

Acknowledgements

My thanks go to all those who have shared their stories and journeys with me, particularly over the last five years.

Particular thanks to the Diocese of Portsmouth and the Diocese of Chester who invited me to speak at their Diocesan Conferences. Those addresses become the foundation of this book.

Thanks also to individuals who read those addresses and encouraged me to keep working on these themes and especially to Jean Hoggard, Abbot Stuart Burns OSB, Norman Ivison, Judy Hirst, Helen Cameron, Rob Marshall, Paul Bayes and Michael Moynagh. Particular thanks as ever to Kathryn Pritchard, Thomas Allain-Chapman and the team at Church House Publishing for their confidence.

Finally, it's been a slightly strange experience to write without footnotes, but my thanks to all those whose writings I have read and whose wisdom has contributed to these pages.